Safe at Home

★

wm

WILLIAM MORROW

An Imprint of HarperCollins*Publishers*

Safe at Home

Confessions of a
Baseball Fanatic

ALYSSA MILANO

SAFE AT HOME. Copyright © 2009 by Alyssa Milano. All rights reserved. Printed in the United States of America. No part of this book may be used or reproduced in any manner whatsoever without written permission except in the case of brief quotations embodied in critical articles and reviews. For information address HarperCollins Publishers, 10 East 53rd Street, New York, NY 10022.

HarperCollins books may be purchased for educational, business, or sales promotional use. For information please write: Special Markets Department, HarperCollins Publishers, 10 East 53rd Street, New York, NY 10022.

FIRST EDITION

Designed by Janet M. Evans

Library of Congress Cataloging-in-Publication Data has been applied for.

ISBN 978-0-06-162510-7

09 10 11 12 13   OV/RRD   10 9 8 7 6 5 4 3 2 1

This book is dedicated to my beautiful parents, Lin and Tom. Thank you for always making me feel safe at home and for the countless sacrifices you made so that I can chase moonbeams.

Contents

Foreword

When I came out west to manage the Dodgers in 2008, I didn't know much about Alyssa Milano. I knew who she was, but I didn't know about her passion for baseball and the Dodgers. I didn't know that she was a familiar face at most of the Dodgers home games.

My introduction did not take long.

One of the Dodgers' most visible and vocal supporters, she's kind of hard to miss for most of us in the dugout. As I began to learn about her love of baseball, I realized that there were certain things we had in common. Like me, she's a former Brooklynite transplanted to Los Angeles. Like me, she's passionate about the Dodgers, but more than that, she's passionate about baseball and its ability to connect her with the past and her family.

Like me, Alyssa has not always been a Dodgers fan. In fact, early on it seemed like she never would be. Her father was from Brooklyn, and as a child he was an avid Dodgers fan. Like so many others from my native borough, his sense of what baseball meant to a city was shaped by what he saw during the years that the Dodgers *were* Brooklyn. His definition of a baseball community was constructed from the beams of the ballpark and the view from the bleachers—a view that I myself was all too familiar with. Understandably, he swore off the Dodgers after Walter O'Malley moved the team out west. It was only through the circumstances of her career that Alyssa and her father found themselves in Los Angeles in the mid-1980s, following the Dodgers and using baseball to bridge the gap between L.A. and their native New York City—the gap between his past and her present. As her father reunited with his team, he began to pass on the vision he'd left behind at Ebbets Field to his daughter.

I, too, grew up in Brooklyn during the most memorable time of baseball in New York. Like Alyssa's father, my vision of what baseball means to a city and a neighborhood was shaped by my earliest memories of life on the side streets off Flatbush Avenue, with players like Jackie Robinson and Sandy Koufax. Though the game has changed a lot since then, I've carried those memories with me to every team and organization that I've been a part of. No matter what my role, I've always been aware of the special relationship between the fans and the team. I've always played and managed knowing full well how important it is for a city to embrace the team, and how crucial it is for baseball to bridge the gap between generations of fans.

Safe at Home not only taps into the spirit and passion of all baseball fans, it also touches on something more universal. This is not just a book for the most die-hard among us; this is a book for everyone—from those who buy the jerseys of their favorite players to those who have never even been to a game. It reaches out to everyone because it's about the role that baseball plays in all of our lives. Once being a fan is in your blood, it's an impossible thing to shake off; and what one takes away from Alyssa's writing is a clearer sense of how the game passes from one generation to the next. Many readers will have similar stories and will relate to how Alyssa feels about baseball and the effect it has had on her family.

Perhaps part of what makes Alyssa's tale so special is that it looks at this generational gift of baseball from a different perspective. All too often when people talk about baseball hand-me-downs from one generation to the next, we talk about fathers and sons, grandfathers and grandsons, and while those moments are important, they only tell half the story. Rarely have sportswriters and historians paid attention to the ever-expanding role that female fans have played in the support and growth of this game. And rarely have the women been able to tell their stories. *Safe at Home* gives a voice to these stories that have always been a part of the game but have only recently emerged to take their rightful place in its history.

In the end, *Safe at Home* is not just a book about the Dodgers and the Yankees or about Los Angeles and New York. It's more than that. To be "safe at home" is not simply to show up at every game and support your team, it's to recognize that your team's ballpark is also a piece of your personal history. And that no matter which players are on the field, they are your connection to a tradition that began many years ago and will, I hope, continue to be passed on from generation to generation.

—Joe Torre

Author's Note

Throughout this book I've made a lot of references to baseball terminology and expressions. While some of you may know these words and expressions, some of you might be left wondering what it all means. To help you through any questions you have, at the back of this book you'll find a glossary that explains many baseball terms. Some of these I use repeatedly; some of them are just things you hear if you spend too much time watching *SportsCenter*. Either way, I hope they're useful and you enjoy them.

Introduction

Some people need yoga to relax. Others turn on Bach's *Goldberg Variations*. Painters paint. Chocolate soothes some, knitting—or a glass of wine, or a crossword puzzle—others. What brings me bliss is a simple sound: the dulcet voice of Vin Scully, calling a Dodgers game. Other women dream of papaya facials and mango pedicures. Give me a hot dog, a pitchers' duel, and a late-inning suicide squeeze, and I melt like hot pine tar.

I'm in love. Not with Vin Scully, though I adore him. Not with the Dodgers, though anyone who wants to kick dirt on Joe Torre's shoes—or Tommy Lasorda's—better be willing to come through me first. I'm in love with baseball. I didn't plan it and I didn't seek it, but it happened. Somehow, without my trying and with me barely knowing, I fell hard.

Isn't that how it always happens?

A romantic would say it started in Staten Island, where I

grew up and where I watched the Yankees on television from the safety of my father's lap. (That my dad let the men in pinstripes even appear in our home proves the tidal pull of the game; Brooklyn-born, he was a lifetime Dodgers fan who still cursed and spat whenever the name O'Malley was uttered in our house, which it usually wasn't.) A romantic would say that the child who falls asleep to the crack of a bat is infected with baseball fever for the rest of her life. But in my case, a romantic would be wrong. So before you decide that mine is the heartwarming tale of a little girl whose life was saved by a fat man pointing toward center field, think again. Growing up, I was not the kid who slept with a glove underneath her pillow. I wasn't the young girl who dreamed of marrying Mickey Mantle (though reporters would later have me romantically linked with everyone from Carl Pavano to Josh Beckett, which I'll get to later). I was just a daughter who loved her father, who loved baseball. Then I was a teenager who loved other things, and I was a working actress living in Los Angeles in the land of the team that broke Dad's heart. Even more mysterious, I was rooting for them.

How'd it happen? Why? When? Those are mysteries as unfathomable as the postseason slumps of Alex Rodriguez. But happen it did. Initially, I was simply rooting for the home team, but then I was rooting for something bigger and more important. Let me be clear here: I don't feel as strongly for any team as I do for the Dodgers. But as much as I love the boys in blue, I love the game more. I love the craft and balletic precision of a 4–6–3 double play, the tension of a full count, the sheer animal joy of a walk-off homer. I love crafty Zen masters like Greg Maddux, aging sluggers like Papi Ortiz, rangy, rawboned flamethrowers like Randy Johnson. I even love the sportswriters who use phrases like "rangy rawboned flamethrowers." (But couldn't they dress better? And did it take the Mitchell Report to persuade them that some of the guys were on the juice? I could tell something was going on after seeing a few of those stegosaurus necks up close.)

I love it all. I love slugging averages and on-base percentage and Whitey Ball and Billy Ball and *Moneyball* and the new breed of technomanager who will tell you that according to the most sophisticated statistical analysis available, David Eckstein is worth more than Nomar Garciaparra. (Which is absolutely insane, but give a certain kind of man a computer and a few volumes of Bill James and his brain starts to liquefy.) I love the leather-faced, flinty-eyed beer vendors who remember the Jurassic era, when Valenzuelas roamed the mounds, and who will gently remind you that it wasn't statistical analysis or computer models that called to a broken-down, gimpy-legged veteran in the bottom of the ninth in a game his team had no business winning; that it wasn't a computer model that dragged his creaky, battered body to the plate; that it wasn't data, or cutting-edge vector analysis, or any newfangled technoanything who with one old-fashioned, panther-hearted, old-school swing changed the course of a World Series and etched his name—in friggin' *granite,* honey—into baseball history.

They say there are three words that will reduce most any

woman on earth to a blubbering heap of joy. With me, it takes only two: "Kirk Gibson."

If you're already a fan, you understand. If you're not, you might wonder what all the fuss is about. Here's what it's about: It's about watching shortstop Khalil Greene twist his body in ways that no mortal should be able to, and to feel gratitude and awe at the majesty of the human spirit; it's about watching pitcher Rick Ankiel suffer a postseason mental breakdown so complete and naked that it makes you feel wonder and pity at the fragility of the human psyche, and compassion for anyone who has ever dreamed big and fallen hard.

It's about autumns of disappointment followed inevitably by hope—and a new batch of live arms—every spring training. It's about snow in Cleveland on opening day, winter trades over imaginary hot stoves in California, and wait till next year. It's about the brutal, irrefutable logic of Erik Bedard's high heat and the way dancing knuckleballs keep an old guy like Tim Wakefield forever young. It's about debating the wisdom of the designated-hitter rule late at night with a beloved and important girlfriend, who would be a lot more beloved and infinitely more important if she would just stop already with her illogical, wingnut arguments in favor of the DH and admit that the National League plays a more pure form of baseball.

It's about how you can always trust a man who hits the cutoff man, and how a guy who watches more than one third strike in a weekend is not a guy you want to take home to meet Mom. It's about whether baseball players make good boyfriends.

What's all the fuss about? It's about a child's game and an adult's joy. It's about winning and losing, steroids and honor, trades and loyalty. It's about the newest stats and the oldest of old-school grit. It's about that sweet spot in a woman's heart where the streets of Staten Island and the boulevards of Hollywood intersect and get all mixed up.

In some ways, the more success I have attained in my career, the smaller my world has become. I'm not complaining, just telling the truth, as anyone who's ever worked in my business will admit. I have a good life, and a lot of people recognize my face, and I'm immensely grateful for both of those things. But my life is not perfect and never has been. Growing up in front of the camera and around Hollywood brings the perks of success, but it also creates problems of its own. Everyone thinks they know you because they watched you get older and saw you age in real time for the last twenty-five years. It's not just people on the street, but most people you meet who are quick to pigeonhole you and assume that you'll conform to their vision of you. A life in the limelight offers the illusion of intimacy while creating the reality of distance. And let's face it: Hollywood is a place where illusions and reality bump up against each other every minute.

"Isn't that what'shisname?" And "Oh, my, hasn't she aged?" And "Did you read what such and such magazine said about so and so, and can you imagine . . . ?"

I've learned to live with all that, and, like I said, I'm not complaining, but as anyone knows who has ever given a speech in public, or pretended to be something she's not, or worried what people think about her, it can be exhausting.

Which is a long way of saying that not only do I love baseball, I love what baseball does for me. It connects me, it relaxes me, and it frees me. When I'm in my regular seat at Dodger Stadium, or watching a game at another ballpark, I'm not worried about what anyone thinks of me, and I'm not paying any attention to what I think of anyone else. I'm not thinking about my next project, or wondering about my work in my last one. When I'm at the ballpark, I'm a fan, just like all the other fans. We're all part of something bigger than any one person. We're not red state or blue state, black or white, Christian or Jew, Hindu or Muslim. We're just fans, bound by our love for the game. And that love travels well. When I'm on the road, baseball is the way I meet people. Ask a stranger about the weather and he's a stranger talking about the weather. Inquire as to his opinion regarding the generation gap in the Dodgers dugout last season, or whether the Cardinals can replace Edmonds in center field, or if A-Rod (his postseason problems notwithstanding) will make everyone forget about Barry Bonds, and that stranger is a friend.

That's what all the fuss is about. It's about how I fell in love with baseball, and how baseball loved me back. And isn't that the way love's supposed to work? What's all the fuss about? It's about a game that changed my life. It's about how it can change yours, too.

chapter *one*

The First Pitch

Let the beauty of what you love be what you do.
—RUMI

I long for the old days my father talks about. The days when kids stuck baseball cards in the spokes of their bicycles and rode the streets of Brooklyn until they came to a stickball game, at which point they jumped off, put their kickstands down, and jumped in. He actually got weepy about it a few years back when he told me of this time (and mind you, it wasn't the first time he told me of this time). He told me about how a city of immigrants welcomed a team of immigrants, and how no other place in the world, and no other team, could have done what *his* team did, which was to hire a black man named Jackie Robinson as its shortstop, and end segregation in baseball.

Was there ever such a Utopia? Were there really streets filled with kids playing games, free, apparently, from Wal-Mart's Corporate America, and all the other things that are part of modern society, as we now know it? My dad says such a world existed, and that its center was Ebbets Field, a magical place where heroes named Robinson and Reese and Campanella and Snider didn't just rule the neighborhood, they lived there, walking the streets and shopping at the corner stores with the rest of the locals. Kids snuck into games under the bleachers, and everyone hated the Yankees because they were cocky and affected and didn't reflect what that era was all about.

"Baseball came of age while our country came of age," he recalled ever so proudly.

Memory is a tricky thing, and the good old days always look good a few decades later. Revisionist history, especially when it comes from a father who never misses an opportunity to discuss what Brooklyn used to be like. But when my dad talked about those days, he gave me a glimpse into a world where men played like kids, and kids played hooky to cheer the men, bought Tootsie Rolls for a nickel, and drank things called egg creams on a big street called Flatbush. It's a far cry from where we find ourselves today. But those differences are all part of the fun.

I was born in Bensonhurst. If you look at a map of Brooklyn, Bensonhurst doesn't seem far away from Flatbush, but apparently, in the seventies, they were worlds apart. My parents were twenty-five years old when I was born, and like most new parents and young couples, they were struggling to make ends meet. In fact, when my parents found out that they were pregnant with me, they had both just lost their jobs.

I never knew of those hardships. The colossal amount of love that they shared for each other and life in general masked those financial struggles well. To this day, forty years after their wedding, their love is the kind that Rumi wrote of. I am, and everything that I've achieved is, a direct extension of that love. Every decision they made after I was born was selfless and in my best interest.

When I was four and crime started to rise in Brooklyn, they left the borough they grew up in and moved the family to Staten Island, where they could fulfill their American dreams of better schools and a safer neighborhood for their daughter. It was hard for both of them to leave the place where they had grown up, a place so inextricably linked to their memories of youth. My father in particular wanted nothing more than for me to enjoy the same egg creams that he had; but that Brooklyn, the Brooklyn of his past, had long since faded, passing into New York's history alongside Ebbets Field and the Polo Grounds.

We lived in a simple house in Staten Island. We didn't have a pool in the backyard or anything extravagant. Our only refuge from the hot humid summers was a fire hydrant on the corner that the locals would open so the kids in the neighborhood could run barefoot through the cascading water and look at the rainbows the water made. (Yes, that idyllic New York City summer image really did happen.) My family didn't have a dishwasher or a rose garden or any luxuries that defined "success." What we had was love and each other. My dad's mom, Nanny Connie, lived downstairs in the apartment that was attached to the humble house. She had plastic slipcovers on her furniture and those thick plastic runners over all the carpet that made funny noises when you dragged your feet on them in that specific way. Nanny Connie would stand me up on a chair and let me knead the dough of whatever Italian pastries she was cooking up from memory, and for dinner she would cook me pastina, which was my favorite food.

My earliest childhood memories are of my mother sketching in her sketchpad (she was a fashion designer at the time) and my father playing the Beatles on the piano or the guitar (he was a musician who gave up his rock-star dream to put food on the table). And there I was, in all of my innocence, donned in a black leotard with pink tights, legwarmers, and ballerina shoes, doing interpretive dance for my audience of Madame Alexander dolls and imaginary friends. I remember the smell of potatoes and eggs on the stove, and when they were ready we would eat them on Wonder bread with ketchup. I remember our brown velvet couch that itched my legs when I sat on it. And . . . I remember on those nights, when creativity and interpretive dance ensued, that off in the corner was our old TV with rabbit ears, and on that TV seemed always to be a Yankees game.

The game on TV was never intrusive. Periodically the reception would hiss and the static would infiltrate the screen.

While the game wasn't always the focus of the night, its presence was constant. Our family coming together with the sounds of umpires, crowd roars, and base hits—not to mention the unforgettably excitable voice of Phil Rizzuto screaming "Holy cow!" like he was sitting on the couch next to you.

Little did I know how much those early days would shape the woman I eventually became. The creativity I was surrounded with back then became the foundation of a career that's now twenty-nine years old. Meanwhile the sport, which started as background noise, grew into a member of the Milano family and became a love of baseball that's now twenty-seven years or so young.

★

I got my first professional acting job when I was seven. I don't know how it happened. I mean, I know the *story* of how it happened, but I don't remember much of the specifics. The story goes like this: My sweet aunt Sissy took me to see the Broadway musical *Peter Pan* for my seventh birthday, and I looked at her all wide-eyed and said, "Aunt Sissy, I can do that." Before anyone knew what happened I was at an open audition for the play *Annie*. Fifteen hundred kids auditioned, and four were picked. I was one of the four. I didn't choose to be an actress. It chose me. I still don't know why it chose me, but I feel blessed for it and this powerful thing called destiny.

My mom and I blissfully toured with the second national touring company of the play, hitting twelve cities in eighteen months. I remember loving it even though it was very hard for me to be away from my father. He would come to visit us. I hated it when he left. My mother, bless her, did the best she could. She tried to make my life as normal as possible. She enrolled me in the Girl Scouts in every city and helped me do my homework; we would read Shel Silverstein's *Where the Sidewalk Ends* out loud, and play jacks on the floor of whatever place we parked the trunk and called home. When the run was coming to an end, my parents asked me what I wanted for a wrap present. "A flute and a brother," I replied.

I got both.

Shortly after I got off the road, my brother, Cory, was born, and it was the best day of my life. Everything was back to normal. We were all together. The Yankees on TV, the sauce cooking on the stove, me creating some fairy tale in my head, and my baby brother screaming his head off in his playpen. The only way Cory could fall asleep was if my mom had the vacuum cleaner on. True story. This led to a lot of vacuuming, and while our house went from clean to immaculate pretty quickly, it became a lot harder to hear the Yankees games on TV.

It was the early eighties, and the Dodgers were long in Los Angeles by then, and every so often Dad would say what a terrible man Walter O'Malley was for stealing the Dodgers and moving them out west. My father's sadness and anger were part of the magic. So was his telling me what a great player Reggie Jackson was, and how if anyone ever tried to boss me around like Yankees manager Billy Martin tried to boss Reggie around, I should do what Reggie did, and tell him no one bossed me, and then go out and hit some more home runs, or something.

I learned how to love and follow the game by watching with my father every night as he propped himself in front of the television set and debated whether Thurman Munson was a better catcher than Yogi Berra. (Tough call.) I was Daddy's little girl, and that meant that he and I could admire Reggie's spirit for the Yankees and feel sad for the loss of the Brooklyn Dodgers together.

It was only years later that I figured out that my dad was all of ten years old when the Dodgers moved from Brooklyn to Los Angeles, and that he wasn't even born when Jackie Robinson took the field as a Dodger and broke the color barrier. It was only later that I puzzled at how his onetime hatred of the Yankees seemed to coexist so very peaceably with his love of all things Reggie. It was only later that I realized that his hatred of the Yankees turned into love when the Dodgers abandoned him, and a community of people just like him, to move to Los Angeles. But that's baseball. That's memory. That's life.

As far as my budding career was concerned, I continued to do theater in New York, pursuing a lot of off-Broadway, small productions in small houses with bigger-than-life people. I learned what it meant to have a strong work ethic, be professional, and say tongue twisters like "The sixth sick sheik's sixth sheep's sick" to warm up my mouth before a live performance. I loved every minute of the creative escape that acting gave me, and also the pride it brought my family. I was an actress because it was a game that I played, and like baseball, it was one I happened to love. I was in the minor leagues and mastering the fundamentals of my sport. Well, as much as any nine-year-old could master anything.

In between jobs, I went to normal public school and continued to audition for roles. My dad used to bring me into work with him in Manhattan when I had auditions. We would take the ferry from Staten Island into the city. He was working as an insurance adjuster at the time and would let me play on the typewriter in the reception area. I would write stories that of course began, "Once upon a time, there was a little girl. . . ." Isn't that how all fairy tales begin? We would walk to my auditions from the office, because people actually walk in New York, and I would point out everyone in a Yankees cap along the way, kind of like punch buggy, only without the buggy. And the punch.

On one of these walks, we ended up at an audition for a pilot called *You're the Boss*. I didn't know what a pilot was, or much of anything special about this pilot other than that the cute guy from *Taxi* was going to be in it and that I was auditioning to play his Italian daughter from Brooklyn. Needless to say, that wasn't much of a stretch for me.

A week after the audition that didn't mean any more than any other audition we got a phone call that changed our lives forever. It was a phone call from my agent informing my parents that ABC wanted to fly me to Los Angeles to audition for the network and with Tony Danza (who will forever be the cute guy from *Taxi* in my eyes). It was a callback for *You're the Boss*.

Had I known at the time what was riding on that audition, I probably would not have been as calm as I was when I got in there. It truly is amazing how resilient children are. I was ten years old, testing for a big television series, and I didn't feel an ounce of the pressure that should come along with such a daunting process. Actually, it wasn't even that exciting for me. What *was* exciting for me was to be in Los Angeles with my dad and taking the back-lot tour of Universal Studios. Now *that* was exciting.

Well, as you probably know, I got that pilot. We shot it in Los Angeles and after what seemed like an eternity and a one-word title change to *Who's the Boss?* we got our pickup for the fall 1983 season.

This was good news, right? Well, yes and no. It was good news for all the obvious reasons, and bad news because it meant that my family had to relocate from the East Coast to the West Coast. My brother was a year old at the time, and my mother had worked her way up as a fashion designer and owned her own store on Eighty-sixth Street. My mother wasn't ready to put her life on hold and fully commit to the move for a gig that was as uncertain as a television show. What if it didn't find an audience and got canceled after the first year? What then? Would we move back to New York? It was a difficult decision, but after a big family meeting, my parents decided that it would be best for my mother and brother to stay in New York until we got some idea of the show's potential. In the meantime, my dad and I would go to Los Angeles.

It's not easy being a kid in Hollywood. (Actually, it's not easy being an adult in Hollywood either, but that's a different story.) But being a child actress out in L.A. is even harder when you have to leave behind one of your parents in order to do it. It was just my dad and me for the first year of the show's eventual eight-season run, and during that time I did everything I could to bond with my father. Neither one of us was accustomed to such a different lifestyle. He was really lost without my mother, and I tried to take care of him. I would cook pastina for him, and no matter how gross it was (and let me tell you, it was gross) he would eat it all up so that I wouldn't feel bad for trying to poison him. On the weekends, we would go to the park, where I would watch him play softball on the *Who's the Boss?* softball team. Tony was the pitcher and my dad was the first baseman. Don Mattingly had nothing on my father.

It was during this year of my life that my father and I created a bond that went beyond just the normal father-and-daughter bond, a bond that still exists to this day. I found solace from the instability of a new environment in his voice. We did fun things together and made up for the time when he wasn't around and it was just my mom and me on the road. This was our time.

And then one afternoon, out of the clear blue sky and with no warning, it happened. Bam! Just like that.

I was in my bedroom in our tiny apartment in Studio City listening to the sound track of *Footloose* on my Walkman. Other than the many pictures of my beautiful mommy and brother, there wasn't really much left of the New York life I once reveled in. I missed them. I missed the way she smelled and I missed his little face. As a kid you don't always have a great idea of the sacrifices your parents make for you, but I knew pretty well what my parents were giving up to let me pursue acting.

My Walkman clicked and it was time to change sides. (God, remember that? When you had to flip the tape over? Insert old-lady joke here.) Anyway, while my headphones were off I heard a noise from the living room. It was a very familiar sound. I walked into the living room and there was my dad, on the couch watching baseball on TV. It was 1984. There was no satellite TV with the baseball package at the time. There was no Internet simulcast or online radio play-by-play. It wasn't the Yankees he was watching. He was watching the Los Angeles Dodgers, and he was loving it.

I casually came up beside him and sat down on the couch. I knew it wasn't the Yankees, but all at once, I saw a look on his face that made me feel like we were back in Staten Island again with the vacuum cleaner running in the other room. I sat down next to him and he began to point things out, telling me how the sound of a wooden bat connecting with a ball could make me feel safe at home when I was three thousand miles away. Other than this occasional game commentary, we didn't speak much while watching the game—we didn't have to, really. All we had to do was watch. Together we comfortably shared the quiet spaces between pitches and the desire for the boys in blue to win.

And so it began. A father and daughter found common ground that day. And even now, baseball connects us. Despite the life experience and time that could have come between us as I grew up and became a woman, despite sometimes not having anything to say, we can always talk about baseball.

On that day back in the early 1980s, baseball and the Dodgers gave me new ways to connect with my father. It wasn't the same as watching the Yankees back in our living room in Staten Island, but it was as close as we were going to get. It was something that we shared as a father and a daughter, something that tied us to home, like the pastina I tried to make, only better because you can't overcook baseball and make it inedible.

When *Who's the Boss?* finally premiered on prime-time television, it was a hit. *Happy Days* was our lead-in—that's how long ago this was (insert old-lady joke here, too). Because of the success of the first season, ABC picked us up for a second season. Once we got that pickup, Mom and Cory moved out to L.A., as did my Nanny Connie, and Aunt Sissy and her son, my cousin Jesse, and then my uncle Mitch, and oh yeah, my mom's friend Janice moved out as well. Everyone took apartments in the same building in Studio City. Once again we were all together.

It's been twenty-four years since then. My immediate family still lives in Los Angeles. My brother and I live together, splitting our time between our condo in Hollywood and our ranch forty miles outside of the craziness. I like to call the ranch the "paparazzi-free zone." Cory is now twenty-six and still needs noise to fall asleep. Thanks to the Dodgers of the eighties having their most successful decade in the club's history, my father is a full-fledged Dodgers fan once more. We've been season ticket holders since 2003, and our seats are right behind the Dodgers dugout. We go to games, watch them on TV, or listen to them on the radio. If we aren't all together we will call, text, or e-mail when something un-fathomable happens. Even now, baseball is the one thing that can connect us no matter how far apart we are.

And during the quieter moments of every game—as the batter walks to the plate or when the pitcher is shaking off the catcher—suddenly I'm back on my father's lap, watching the Yankees of the late seventies and hearing stories about the Dodgers of the fifties. Playing my part in a generational loop that goes back a few grandparents, probably all the way back to the day Abner Doubleday threw out a ball.

As baseball has changed and grown over the years, I have, too. I've come a long way from Bensonhurst to Hollywood. And yet, oddly, I am pretty much the same. I'm still the eight-year-old on that itchy couch in Staten Island, listening to my dad's tales of the greedy villain O'Malley. All of which is my way of saying that I come by my nostalgia honestly. I love my family. I love baseball. And . . . I am still looking for my happily ever after.

chapter two

Our Pastime's Past Time

History is merely a list of surprises. It can only
prepare us to be surprised yet again.

—KURT VONNEGUT

*a*nyone who falls in love with the game as a child can't help it: She's nostalgic. I'm focused on the present—especially if I'm in my seat during a late-summer game and the Dodgers are contending—and I'm thinking about the future—whether it's a role I'm trying to land, or how Manny Ramirez is going to put some more punch into the middle of the Dodger lineup; but part of me is always mucking about the past.

That explains why I tell Cory, when he's going on about how great a pitcher Derek Lowe is, that yeah, he's not bad, but he's no Orel Hershiser. It's the same thing my dad would do, when he would tell me about the Dodger greats of long ago like Duke Snider and Pee Wee Reese. We learn the game as kids, and something gets hardwired in us about the glories of the past, whether it's ours or our parents'.

But even that doesn't explain how baseball inspires *such* reverence for the old days. I'm a sports fan in general, and follow football and hockey and basketball, and I can talk about Joe Namath and Wayne Gretzky and Michael Jordan as enthusiastically as the next girl (or guy), but it's not the same as baseball. I can tell you how many homers Stan "The Man" Musial hit in his last season (12, when he was forty-two years old) and Ernie Banks's lifetime batting average (.274), and when someone says "Let's play two!" just like Banks did before every game—doubleheader or not—I know she isn't just expressing an appetite for work, but a delight in the work she's chosen.

Maybe it's because the game itself is so old, or because almost everyone has a parent or grandparent who will gladly describe the joys of watching Willie Mays make that catch running back to the wall of the Vic Wertz fly ball in deep center field in the Polo Grounds in 1954. Maybe it's because unlike hockey, or basketball, where you have to focus every second, in case you miss something, watching a baseball game is a leisurely, slow-paced affair, and the relaxed speed allows announcers like Vin Scully to fill the gaps in the action with stories from the old days.

Baseball is all about stories. I love those stories. And I've heard enough of them that I try to pay respect to the men who made them possible. Every baseball fan has his own set of baseball stories that help him connect with the past, and I'm no different. Being a true fan means paying respect to the legends of yore. I'm not just talking about walking the hallowed halls of Cooperstown once in your baseball-following life. I'm talking about knowing what the game has stood for throughout its history, what its best players have meant to every era that they've played in, and what they mean today.

Here's one way I pay respect: When I arrive at Dodger Stadium, I park in my usual spot, and then we walk behind home plate, to the Dugout Club. That's one of my favorite moments at the ballpark, because it's in the club that there's a huge floor-to-ceiling picture of Jackie Robinson, and he's smiling. I take the two steps down to the picture and I lift my right arm and say, "Hi, Jackie," and I rub his belly four times, clockwise, and then we go to our seats.

This ritual is not just about being superstitious (though I, like many fans, definitely have a superstitious streak). This ritual is about giving yesterday's greats their due. Baseball history is ongoing—one season picking up where the previous left off. Before I can settle in and cheer, I rub the belly of maybe the greatest Dodger of all, the man who broke the color barrier and changed baseball forever. There I am, an Italian American, an actor born on one coast, working on another, remembering the son of a sharecropper, born in Georgia, still living in baseball memories around the world.

When I'm done bowing to the altar of Jackie Robinson I get to my seat, and there I am, yelling encouragement at players like Russell Martin, Matt Kemp, and James Loney, whom I've watched since they were rookies. Generations removed from the legend yet still part of the elaborate folds of Dodger history. As my brother and I watch a game, we talk about former greats, like Sandy Koufax and Don Drysdale, whom we never saw but feel like we know.

We are all there, fans from everywhere, cheering fuzz-faced rookies, remembering legends dead and alive, listening to play-by play men tell tales of a time before we were born. I know people who struggle with faith, who have a hard time believing there's any kind of benign force in the universe, any sort of order or connective tissue that binds us. I've gone through setbacks myself, struggled with staying optimistic. I don't know anyone who hasn't. We're human. The place that restores me is the ballpark. The place where I reconnect with the past is Dodger Stadium. The image that reminds me that we all have a capacity for justice and love, that we're all in this together, is that picture of Jackie Robinson.

We all have our moments in the game that seem to define the sport for us. For some people, Roger Maris's record-breaking 61st home run was a thing of reverence. For others, the game when Rickey Henderson stole his 939th base, surpassing Lou Brock on the all-time list, is the one to remember. While both of those are amazing achievements, it's not just the records that define my personal baseball lore. What I crave from the past are the moments when baseball became something more than a game, when it stood for something that still resonates.

On September 4, 1993, Yankees left-handed pitcher Jim Abbott threw a no-hitter against the Indians. There have been 256 no-hitters in major-league history, an average of about two per season, but Abbott's game goes beyond the box score and teaches us about the long road to success.

Abbott was born without a right hand. When he pitched, he would rest a glove on his right forearm, and after releasing the ball, he would slip his left hand into the glove and be ready to field just as quickly—if not quicker—than two-handed pitchers. If a ball did come his way, he'd snag it, cradle the glove between his torso and right arm, grab the ball out of the glove with his left hand, and throw to the appropriate bag. It all happened in a blink. Even double plays were turned with precision and quickness.

To say that lots of people would never have thought this possible is an understatement. Most would have doubted his ability to pitch seven innings, let alone an entire game. While many viewed Abbott as disabled, he spent his career trying to turn that perception on its ear. And on that late-summer day in the Bronx, Abbott did just that, becoming the graceful prototype of the will to win. The Indians' lineup that day featured sluggers Albert Belle, Manny Ramirez, and Jim Thome. Sitting them down was no small feat, not to mention the rest of the order: Sandy Alomar Jr., o-for-1. Kenny Lofton, o-for-3. Carlos Baerga, o-for-4. Jim Abbott was unconquerable, in all his one-handed glory.

Any woman will tell you it takes a lot of years dressed in

her own skin to surrender to the fact that, for better or for worse, it's the only skin she will ever have. Jim Abbott's no-hitter came when I was a couple months shy of my twenty-first birthday, a time in my life when I felt like all my insecurities were on constant display. The never-ending refrain going through my head every time I looked in the mirror sounded something like this: I am bowlegged. I am short. My hair is too curly. My arms are too hairy.

Like most women, these insecurities had been bouncing around my head for years. They were plentiful and pretty much dominated my self-image until . . . I watched Jim Abbott's no-hitter. This was a guy born without a right hand, and I was insecure about my hairy arms? Not only that, but here was a guy doing more with one hand than I had ever done with two or could ever do with four. Pitching that day, he was so secure within his body and ability, which gave him the confidence necessary to win. I longed for that kind of self-assuredness, but seeing it embodied in his effort, suddenly I began to think about my own body differently. All I could think about was that if he could find a way to pitch in spite of his body, I should really stop worrying about my bowlegs.

But Abbott's no-hitter meant more to me than just superficial reassurance. It also came at a time when I was young enough to still believe in a thing called hope, but old enough to doubt its influence. That day I came to believe in the influence that hope could have on a life. Abbott's performance proved to me something that my father spent a lifetime trying to teach me: The human spirit is unconquerable.

In the end, Abbott's no-hitter is one of many that have been thrown through the years. He didn't break any records that day, but he did set a new standard of what is possible in this game. He showed all of us who follow the sport that as much as we try to predict the outcome of things and impose limitations on the players we revere, there's always a player somewhere who's waiting to throw our expectations a curveball. (Sorry, sorry, pun totally intended, I just had to put that in there, but I promise it will be the only time in this book that I do that . . . probably.)

Baseball has a rhythm. Throw, hit, run . . . players do this six days a week for six months, not to mention the month and a half of spring training and month of postseason play. So when that rhythm is interrupted, fans notice. They notice it the same way they would a skipped heartbeat, or a pop star forgetting the words to the national anthem. Whether it's an amusing hiccup, like a mascot losing its head, or truly weird, like pitchers swapping each other's wives, or even something tragic, like a premature death that reminds us how terribly human our heroes are, the unexpected moments of the greatest game in the world make us appreciate its rhythms that much more. In these Wild Pitch sections I'll give you the best of the off-key notes throughout baseball history that make us appreciate the symphony of baseball all the more. . . .

Wild Pitch **Boys Among Men**

In 1887, Fred Chapman became the youngest professional baseball player when he played his first and only game for the Philadelphia Athletics at the ripe age of fourteen years, 240 days. He started and pitched five innings, giving up eight hits and four earned runs in what would be a no-decision. He also went 0–for–2 at the plate. Chapman remains the youngest ever major-league participant.

Joe Nuxhall, one year Fred Chapman's senior (at the age of fifteen), is the youngest in the modern era. In 1944, much of the Cincinnati Reds' roster was involved in military service. The Reds were, at first, more interested in Nuxhall's father, but once they feasted their eyes on young Joe, standing six foot two and weighing 190 pounds, attention quickly became focused on the barely pubescent pitcher. While Reds management intended to wait until school was out to bring Nuxhall on board, the Reds' roster was so thin that Nuxhall was on the field for Opening Day, with the principal's permission, of course. Finally, on June 10, the Reds trailed the first-place St. Louis Cardinals 13–0, and in the ninth inning, in came Nuxhall. It wasn't pretty. Yes, he got the first guy to ground out, but five walks, two hits, one wild pitch, and five runs later, Nuxhall was relieved. Though he wouldn't return to the big leagues until 1952, when he was twenty-three, he became an All-Star twice over in 1955 and 1956.

★

What can I say, drama moves me. It probably won't surprise you then that another one of my favorite moments in baseball history is Lou Gehrig's famous speech. I think it's impossible to hear that speech and not get the chills. I don't care if you like baseball or not. Curling could be your national pastime and you would still have to be moved by those words. That speech is about a lot more than baseball.

Despite the strength in his voice, Gehrig's message on July 4, 1939, was a grim one. His baseball career was over, yes, but it was even deeper than that. Less than a month earlier, on June 16, Gehrig was diagnosed with amyotrophic lateral sclerosis, a disease that now bears his name. It is a heartbreaking illness that causes the strong to go weak with muscle atrophy and the degeneration of the central nervous system. Still today there is no cure.

Footage from that day shows Gehrig accepting gift after gift from everyone in the park—baseball VIPs all the way to the groundskeepers. It shows him taking the gifts, then immediately setting them on the ground, because he didn't have the strength to hold them. It shows more than sixty thousand fans celebrating a man who had just lost his livelihood and would soon lose his life, but radiated love and graciousness in spite of it all.

The Yankees retired Gehrig's number 4 that day, making him the first player in major-league history to have a number retired. When it was Yankees manager Joe McCarthy's turn to speak, he said to Gehrig, "It was a sad day in the life of everybody who knew you when you came into my hotel room that day in Detroit and told me you were quitting as a ballplayer because you felt yourself a hindrance to the team. My God, man, you were never that."

Not one to stand on ceremony for too long, Gehrig, after hearing people speak of him, finally got up to say a few words himself. His speech in front of the crowd at Yankee Stadium on Independence Day is one that we've probably all heard and imitated: distorted by static, crisp in its emotion, everlasting in its echo.

Today . . . today . . . today . . . I consider myself . . . myself . . . myself . . . the luckiest man . . . man . . . man . . . on the face of the earth . . . earth . . . earth.

In the history of oratory, his speech was a short one, a mere 276 words. But it's the reality behind those words that gives the speech a poignancy that still resonates today. His words highlighted a selflessness and a perspective that few in the game have ever mustered. Gehrig was a man of massive hitting and fielding skills who was overshadowed by the only player in the game capable of being bigger than the spotlight itself: Babe Ruth, Gehrig's teammate. Still, spotlights weren't in Gehrig's interest. He worked hard—every day—despite the attention he did or did not receive. His streak of 2,130 consecutive games played was the longest such streak until Cal Ripken Jr. broke it some fifty-six years later.

Gehrig's production slipped a little in 1938, and when he continued to struggle during the first eight games in 1939, Gehrig took himself out of the lineup. Team first. Spotlight second, if ever.

We know now that Gehrig's farewell that day in the Bronx was the speech of a dying man, yet he spoke only about his fortunes and how much he had to live for. Less than two years later, on June 2, 1941, Gehrig died. He was thirty-seven.

It's easy to get all misty-eyed about Lou Gehrig; after all, he embodied all that is good—not just in baseball but in sport. But his story becomes even more powerful when you think about the game today and how certain athletes waste few opportunities to flaunt their various injuries and ailments. I mean, guys will go on the fifteen-day DL for a buttocks contusion. Have you ever looked up the word "contusion"? It's a bruise!

As with most defining moments in baseball history, thinking about Lou Gehrig offers a contrast between past and present that seems stark no matter what year it is. I think very highly of today's ballplayers, what they endure, and what they have to put up with from the media. I also think there are a number of reasons present-day baseball players aren't made of the tenacious stuff the past players were made of. The most obvious of those reasons is money. Management and owners don't force their players to play hurt, even if the team needs them to win, because they are protecting their multimillion-dollar investment.

I will say this, though: There is a difference between being hurt and being injured. If a guy is injured, he obviously shouldn't play. If a guy is hurt like with, oh, let's say, a buttocks contusion—he needs to bite the bullet and get his bruised ass on the field. Simply put, I'm not sure they make 'em like Lou Gehrig anymore. I daresay we won't see anyone as selfless as Gehrig again.

If I'm going to respect Gehrig for showing up to work every day, I have to show respect to Ripken, the Iron Man, who bested Gehrig's consecutive-game streak in 1995. He played sixteen seasons straight as a member of the Baltimore Orioles. That's three more seasons than Gehrig. And as Gehrig played through his share of injuries, so too did Ripken.

Now I know you doubters out there love to say that baseball is not a contact sport like football or hockey. "You don't get tackled and hit in baseball, what's the big deal about playing in consecutive games when the risk of injury is so low, blah blah blah."

Such arguments are way too superficial. True, baseball is not a contact sport like football, but it is just as physically demanding. Ripken spent most of his streak at shortstop but played some at third base, too. If you know anything about the organization of the field, you know that both of these positions put him in the path of some of the game's hardest-hit line drives and hopping mad grounders. Instead of linebackers heading your way, it's a small ball traveling faster than a NASCAR auto.

Not enough, you say? Well, think about this: Of all the positions in the infield, shortstop is the most physically demanding. As shortstop your mobility is the key to making strong throws across the diamond to first and turning the most common of double plays, the 6–4–3, with outsized acrobatics. The shortstop must battle players coming in hard to second, handle balls taking funny hops, and dive into the stands to catch foul balls. They have to be able to do it all. Whereas with good pitching the outfielders can go a couple of innings without seeing a ball hit their way, the shortstop rarely has that luxury. Even if the shortstop has a strong starter on his side, he still gets a workout. He's involved in play inning in and inning out.

But that's not even the best part of what Ripken did. The real beauty of Ripken's feat was that he accomplished it while being a Gold Glove shortstop. He didn't do a mediocre job or just enough to keep his streak alive. On the contrary, for 2,632 straight games, Ripken darted right, lunged left, ran in, and pedaled back for anything hit his way. He was one of the best in the league. Not once did Ripken start a game as the designated hitter. As a shortstop, he jumped over incoming base runners attempting to break up double plays, and as a third baseman, he repeatedly had to endure opponents' high spikes. At the plate, Ripken was often in the heart of the order, so he had to swing a productive bat. It's one thing to show up. It's another thing entirely to perform at a high level. And Ripken did it.

So on September 6, 1995, Cal Ripken Jr. surpassed Lou Gehrig's consecutive-game streak when he took the field at home against the California Angels. I remember watching it on ESPN, and most of the country tuned in too. I thought it was fitting in a storybook kind of way when he hit that home run in the bottom of the fourth. It was like the baseball gods wanted something good to happen, a moment in which baseball fans could set on a pedestal and honor with pride the achievement that comes after determination. And when the game became official in the top of the fifth, the banners on the warehouse beyond the right-field wall at Camden Yards changed from 2,130 to 2,131, signifying in large black numbers how hard this man had worked. Ripken ran an impromptu lap around the stadium at that moment, shaking hands with fans, reminding people watching everywhere that we'd all been a part of something good.

Ripken's achievement, like Gehrig's and Abbott's, is the kind that makes you reconsider life outside the diamond. While each has played its own significant role in breaking fans' preconceived notions of what's possible, for my money, there's only one game that comes to mind when thinking of contests that shaped life outside the base paths: Jackie Robinson's first major-league game.

Yeah, okay, so my most hallowed moment of baseball history happens to involve a Dodger, but honestly, this one is hard to argue against. America was bitterly divided in 1947. The issue, on some levels, was as simple as black and white. The country tried to navigate itself around racial lines, and segregation was in full swing. White people over here; black people over there.

And then, on April 15, 1947, Jackie Robinson took the field for the Brooklyn Dodgers, the first time an African American was allowed to play in the majors since 1889. By breaking the color barrier of the nation's premier sport, Jackie made a stand against racial injustices, challenged so-called established beliefs and practices, and forced the country to take a long, hard look at itself.

By no means was Jackie's journey easy. He and his family endured loads of hate mail, death threats, and ill-tempered fans while on the road, not to mention having to stay in separate hotels when traveling with the team.

Jackie's rookie year was still sixteen years before Martin Luther King Jr. marched to the steps of the Lincoln Memorial and told the country about his dreams in 1963. Jackie, in fact, played his entire career before King's speech, retiring after the 1956 season. Indeed, Jackie took the first steps in the American civil rights movement, a point that emphasizes the pressure he was under. If he had failed, segregation would have won. If he had failed, he would have proven to all the bigots and racists that they were right the entire time. But he didn't fail. Jackie hit .297 with 12 home runs and a National League–leading 29 stolen bases. He ranked fifth in the Most Valuable Player voting and took home the Rookie of the Year Award in its first year of existence. Baseball never looked back (though it may have dragged its feet: Jackie also ranked second in the NL by being hit by pitches nine times); and the leaders of the country took notice.

In 1997, Jackie's uniform number 42 was retired across all Major League Baseball teams. Only those players wearing the number at the time could continue wearing it. The Yankees' Mariano Rivera is the last player to don number 42. At some point he'll retire, and there will be no more 42s in baseball. And no matter how outstanding their careers, only one 42 will be immortal—a player from the past, whose grace and courage reminds us how far we've come and how far we still have to go.

Every season, there will be numerous games that stand out as statistical achievements. Pitchers will record strike-out records, hitters will reach batting average goals. There's no denying these benchmarks, but they are not the truly memorable moments in my baseball lore. Bringing up all these revered names from the past, I'm not sure what it says about my tastes that my favorite moments are those that make the game, not to mention sport in general, greater.

Much like each of us has a personal history that is unique to his or her own experience, baseball history can be relevant to our own lives. For me, the most important are those games that still mean something if you strip away all the numbers. They are the games that still matter regardless of who's playing and what team you support. They are the games that remind me of the human spirit's innate ability to prevail. These are the games that truly resonate because they are the ones that inspire me in my life away from baseball. They call me to be a better person or stop me when I start feeling sorry for myself. They remind me of how we've grown as a nation or show me that my personal growth is a never-ending work in progress. These are the games that deserve a place on baseball's altar.

Moments like these don't happen every day, and that's why I make it a point to bring them up, to dust them off every year and talk about them with other fans, so that I'm drawing a connection between the past and present. These stories can remind me why I continue to follow this sport year in and year out.

As a fan, I don't expect a Jim Abbott or a Cal Ripken to come along more than once, but what keeps me watching is the notion that somewhere there's a sixteen-year-old kid who is going to do something amazing that will once again challenge what we all thought was possible.

chapter three

Heroes and Villains

Less than a foot made the difference
between a hero and a bum.

—GROVER ALEXANDER

*L*et me tell you a story. (It's a quick story, I promise, not to mention that it's completely inappropriate for bedtime, as it has swearing, drunken Billy Martin ramblings, and George Steinbrenner. As you probably know, any story with Steinbrenner is automatically disqualified as bedtime material.)

In 1977, Reggie Jackson came to the Yankees as the most expensive free agent signed to date (though his five-year, $2.96 million salary looks paltry by our modern standards). For almost all of that season he was, without a doubt, one of the most disliked members of the Yankees, and probably one of the most unpopular people in all of New York. Why? Because for the first several months of his career as a Yankee he failed to perform at the level that was expected of him. Instead, he went out, bought expensive fur coats, and displayed a penchant for New York nightlife.

It was a tumultuous season for many reasons, but Reggie's consistent underachievement played no small part. In some of the press he was demonized, cast in the role of underperforming man about town, the kind of guy who knows how to go out and spend his salary, but seems to have forgotten why he was getting paid it in the first place. In other parts of the New York media he was revered for his quick wit and for the clear talent that was lingering beneath the pressure of playing in front of an audience that made his previous home of Oakland look tiny. His tussles with manager Billy Martin were legendary, pushing to the brink of physical conflict, or as some might say, going over the line.

Martin, a renowned Yankee in his own right, only added to the tension of the situation. By all accounts he was hitting the booze a lot that season, and while this wasn't much different from any other season, having Reggie on the team was. Reggie brought with him the weight of expectation, and the pressure of being a New York manager with an underperforming star player did not sit well with Martin. It also didn't help that he had George Steinbrenner breathing down his neck every step of the way, always second-guessing his choices and making it clear that Martin's head was always on the chopping block.

The end result was that Martin was irritable, cantanker-ous, and downright nasty (more so than usual), but in this persona, he proved the perfect media foil for Reggie: Martin, the hard-living, hard-drinking working-class manager, the counterweight to Reggie's overpaid and underproductive talent. Together they made a striking pair—the wiry under-dog of a manager and his imposing tower of a player. Chances were that if you liked one of them, you didn't like the other. On any given day one was the hero and one was the villain. Sometimes they were both.

For the entire season it went like that. In a sport that had seen plenty of contentious relationships between managers and players, theirs set a new record for vitriol and acrimony, playing out every day in grand form across the back pages of the *New York Post* and the New York *Daily News*.

But all that changed with a swing of the bat. Actually, it was more like three swings. I may not need to tell you where it all went from there.

One night in October, Game 6 of the World Series to be precise, Reggie Jackson hit three home runs, on three con-secutive first pitches, helping the Yankees with Billy Martin, ire and all, to their first World Series in fifteen years. All at once, Reggie became permanently etched in Yankee lore. Sud-denly the man who had been intermittently ridiculed by the city of New York for the entire season was the greatest Yankee hero since Mantle hung up his spikes in the 1960s.

I mention this well-worn tale of Reggie and Billy, not be-cause it's new, but because it perfectly embodies the kind of stories that make every baseball season worth following.

Each season presents a full story—complete with a beginning, a middle, and an end, and a range of characters, personalities, and feuds that make the game what it is. Each season is one long soap opera complete with backstabbing, bad-mouthing, blame shifting, and glory hogging. Usually the characters duel it out on the field and not in their clubhouse against each other, but it's the unpredictability of the game that gives every season its own unique place in baseball's history.

To be clear, I'm not talking about bench-clearing brawls and pitchers hitting batters on purpose; what I'm talking about is something more cosmic than all that. Good versus Evil. Heroes versus Villains. These are the forces that make baseball fans get up in the morning.

Every season is a story in its own right, and like any good story, it has a cast of characters that you follow all the way to October (hopefully). Regardless of your team's win-loss record, any season worth following will have its share of both heroes and villains; ideally, the heroes are on your team and the villains are not, but life is rarely that neat.

That hitter on your division rival who always manages the two-out single against your closer with a pinch runner on second (Eric Byrnes, the Dodger killer for me). That pitcher who routinely shows up your entire lineup even though his best pitch is a knuckleball that moves so slowly you're pretty sure you could hit it. (Charlie Haeger, the relief pitcher for the Padres—seriously, who brings in a knuckleballer in relief? That's just mean.) Or the pitcher on your team who never plays up to his $15-million-per-year price tag (Jason Schmidt). These are the guys that are hard to root for.

The guys that are easy to root for . . . well, they're pretty obvious, not just because they're talented but because they're the kind of players you want to like. They're the people that you react to because there's something almost genetic inside you that says you must. You have little choice in the matter—not just because of *what* they produce but because of *how* they produce. They complement their skills with a class that you don't find everywhere. They're the players that show up game in and game out, play hard, and never seem to let you down.

The amazing thing about the players on each end of the spectrum is that they're always in the eye of the beholder and the context of the season. All it takes for some villains to become heroes is going 3-for-4 on the second-to-last game of the season when your team is in wild card contention. Suddenly the player who underperformed the entire year re-writes the story and goes down as the guy who came through when it counted. Similarly, and less dramatically, a phone call right before the impending trade deadline can turn your hero into a villain as the player you learned to love suddenly becomes a first baseman on the other side of a rivalry.

Usually the conflicts are less volatile and dramatic than what went on with Reggie and Billy in '77, but never underestimate how a swing of the bat or striking out the side in the bottom of the eighth can invert all the forces of good and evil in this game.

Okay, okay, maybe the word "good" should be reserved for people who help teach homeless children to read while saving animals from unnecessary medical testing. And maybe "evil" is supposed to be used on . . . well . . . I won't even go there. So having good guys and bad guys in baseball is a bit irrational, but guess what? Being a fan is a bit irrational. (Okay, it's quite irrational and very emotional.)

If I were a less emotional person, I wouldn't have booed and screamed at my television every time Barry Bonds stepped to the plate in the 2001 season, calling him names, telling him he was going to strike out, working myself into such a state that at least once, my mom called out from the next room to see if I was okay.

If I were a more calculating, purely-by-the-numbers baseball analyst, I wouldn't have felt chills down my spine at the 2008 All-Star Game in New York City's Yankee Stadium, watching former bad boy and drug addict Josh Hamilton smack 28 home runs out of the park in the first round of the Home Run Derby. I screamed then too—with joy—and grabbed my little brother, who was standing next to me, and shook his arm and demanded to know, was he *watching,* could he *believe* that, wasn't that the most astonishing act of redemption he had ever *seen,* the most vivid example of the human spirit's resilience and beauty?!

If I were a more logic-driven kind of person, I might admit that Barry Bonds is just a highly accomplished, incredibly driven athlete who's still worthy of admiration despite his reputation. If I were more calm and steely eyed, I might say Josh Hamilton is simply a young guy who had to go through some hard times, and some bad behavior, before he wised up.

But here's the thing: I *am* emotional and I'm not all that calculating. So even though I know in my head that people are complicated, that baseball players are, after all, just doing a job, I still want to think of them in terms of right and wrong. It's primitive, but fans have been this way since the beginning of the game. Dizzy Dean and Lefty Grove were saints, grandparents tell their grandchildren, but oh, that Ty Cobb, he was a *bad* man. Today, instead of the racist, misanthropic Cobb, we have the gambling Pete Rose and the steroid-accused Bonds. The story of Josh Hamilton transforms into a magical tale, the stirring arc of a man's rise from the hell of hopelessness and addiction to the sweet, rarefied air of clean living and deep faith and 28 home runs.

Here's the other thing, the bigger thing: *All* fans are emotional. All fans I know, even those with slide rules for hearts, get caught up in the game. Why do you think people in Baltimore still applaud whenever Cal Ripken walks into a restaurant there? Why do you think Boston fans still refer to a certain Yankee shortstop not by his given name, but as Bucky Fucking Dent? Why do fans in ballparks (and on couches in front of televisions, and leaning forward in armchairs, radios by their side) from the Redwood Forest to the Gulf Stream waters scream themselves hoarse every summer?

I'll tell you why. Because no matter how complicated our lives get, how filled with doubt and uncertainty and nuance and the small and inevitable disappointments of adulthood, the game is always a place we can return to, where rules are clear and there are winners and losers, sinners and saints.

It's a place where effort and skill prevail, where if you do your best, and play your hardest, and work hard, everything will be all right.

Wild Pitch The Real Heroes and Villains

On September 23, 1978, Lyman Bostock, an outfielder for the Angels who was entering his prime in his fourth big-league season, was murdered after a game against the White Sox.

We hear these stories once in a while, often enough that we become desensitized to the tragedy: young man, entering his athletic prime, a bullet cuts his life short. But the Bostock murder still found a way to hurt us not because of what he could have been, but because of what he seemed destined to be. He was becoming the good face of the game at a time when players were greedy. He was to be an ambassador of the sport.

In the beginning of the 1978 season, under the pressure of playing in his first season with a new team for what was big money in those days, Bostock struggled—his April average was so low (.150 in fact) that he tried to return that month's salary to Angels owner Gene Autry. Autry refused, so Bostock donated it to charity. *Wow.*

At the time of his death, Bostock was hitting .296, for a short, four-year career average of .311. After going 2–for–4 against the White Sox, Bostock left Chicago to visit his uncle in Gary, Indiana. After dinner at a family home, Bostock and his uncle gave a ride to a friend and her sister, Barbara Smith. Unbeknownst to anyone, Smith's estranged husband trailed them in a car. He pulled up next to them at an intersection and, jealous over the fallacious assumption that Barbara was romantically involved with Bostock, fired his shotgun into the car. The target was Barbara, but Bostock was struck in the temple. He was dead at twenty-seven. The gunman was found not guilty by reason of insanity and underwent psychiatric treatment for seven months.

Tonya Moore knows what it's like to be a target. She was the wife of All-Star relief pitcher Donnie Moore. Moore had a thirteen-year career in the bigs, playing for the Chicago Cubs, St. Louis Cardinals, Milwaukee Brewers, Atlanta Braves, and California Angels.

It is said that Moore never got over his loss in Game 5 of the 1986 American League Championship Series against the Boston Red Sox. He was one strike away from the AL pennant. Instead, with two outs and two strikes in the ninth, Moore gave up a two-run walk-off homer to Dave Henderson. The Angels lost that game, and Boston won the next two, advancing to the World Series against the Mets.

Flash forward to 1989, when Moore was re-leased by the Omaha Royals, a Triple-A team, when his agent filed a grievance saying Moore owed him $75,000, and when his marital problems consumed him. On July 18, after consuming copious amounts of drugs and alcohol, he shot his wife, Tonya, three times at their Anaheim home in front of their three children. One daughter fled and drove Tonya to the hospital, where she survived the gunshots. But still at home and in front of one of his two sons, Moore shot and killed himself.

★

For many people, Barry Bonds was a villain out of central casting. Standoffish with reporters, accused of doping, and unapologetic about his motivations, he certainly didn't appear to care whether you rooted for him or not. He was the ambassador of the Me-Only era of sports, the team be damned. His alleged demands to travel on private jets and stay in different hotels than his teammates didn't win fans in his clubhouse or the front office. And then there was his showboating. After hitting a home run, no matter what the score, he'd stand at the plate, watch it sail into the stands, slowly trot around the bases, then walk as he crossed home plate, pointing to the sky or God or whatever it is that he believes in. It irritates me even now just to think about it. All of this without mentioning those gaudy hoop earrings he'd wear and those stupid wristbands with his headshot on them. His whole display had way too much ego for my taste (keep in mind, I work in Hollywood, so I'm well versed in how people display their egos).

It's not a stretch of the imagination to wonder why someone might dislike Barry Bonds. With him, everything is/was fodder. For better or for worse, though, his negative presence did fill a role. Bonds was the face of *Game of Shadows*–era baseball. He's the archetype of a sports star pushed too far in search of his own personal glory. His quest for himself came at the expense not just of his team but of the game. Whether or not he used drugs, the popular perception of him is that he's the quintessential example of someone who juiced to get ahead.

Perhaps what made Bonds such a target for criticism was not just his attitude, but that of the man whose record Bonds was eclipsing. For many (myself included), Hank Aaron was a man who epitomized all that was right and just in the game. Aaron came to the majors in 1954, still early in the march toward integration. His career unfolded naturally, which is to say his prime wasn't interrupted by war or shortened by segregation. Fans of the day got to see the best of him, from day one. With the media, he was shy and soft-spoken, and his personality seemed rather unremarkable. In short, he just seemed like a pleasant person to be around. How could you *not* root for him? It must have been so natural to cheer when he came to the plate.

Whereas Aaron's possession of baseball's greatest record showed just how amazing baseball can be, Bonds's attitude toward the record seemed to be about one thing: Barry

Bonds. Whether or not that was true is hard to say, but this evident attitude gave me all the more reason to see him in a negative light. While the steroid accusations certainly made people question the legitimacy of the record, where Bonds truly failed in my eyes was in his arrogance at replacing a legend. He came to see himself as being bigger than the game, bigger than the game's history; he was the entire story as opposed to just a part of it.

Though Bonds appeared to have mixed feelings about his infamous legacy, usually the best antagonists are not only okay with being villains, they embrace it. George Steinbrenner may be the best example of this behavior, a man who during his tenure at the helm of the Yankees showed little hesitation when it came to criticizing and alienating his players and managers. His clashes with Martin are well documented and frequently revisited. But when casting Steinbrenner as a scoundrel, why doesn't anyone mention his illegal contributions to Richard Nixon's campaign that Watergate revealed? Look it up. He was suspended from baseball in 1974 for that revelation, and then again in 1990 for another shady episode in hiring a private investigator to dig up dirt on slugger Dave Winfield.

Really, though, his feuds are epic beyond comedy. He managed to insult Yogi Berra, whom he fired after Berra had managed only sixteen games for the 1985 Yankees, to such an extent that Berra didn't return to the stadium for fourteen years. Fourteen years! C'mon, his name is Yogi. Okay, Lawrence, but everyone calls him Yogi, and how can you not find common ground with a man named Yogi? Then there was the time Steinbrenner tried to take away Yankees employees' dental insurance in 2003. It never happened, but his intentions were there and were leaked to the New York City press, prompting a firestorm of protest.

Like Bonds, Steinbrenner too filled a purpose in each year's baseball drama. If the Yankees were winning he'd be eerily silent, but the second the Red Sox began to gain ground, people watched and waited, wondering what he was going to do or say next. Everyone would parse his words trying to figure out whether the manager or the second baseman was history. They'd read his released statements like tea leaves, in the way that bankers try to anticipate a rate cut by the Fed.

Today Steinbrenner has fallen from public view, with his sons controlling day-to-day operations of the team. Still, his charismatic ownership put its stamp on the game. He bought the beleaguered franchise in 1973 for a paltry $10 million. Even if you adjust for inflation, that's an absurdly low sum for one of professional sports' most storied franchises. Anyway, he took that investment and spun it into the single biggest brand in all of professional sports. Some people might say that regardless of everything else he did, that legacy itself was his most dastardly deed. He spent more on players than anyone else, and he had no problem making the future of their careers gossip for sports journalists. Yes, Steinbrenner spent a lot of money on players he thought could win, but boy did he ever take it out on the dogs when things didn't go right.

Like the Steinbrenners of the game, the good guys who

become ensconced in the pantheon of greats usually have to embrace their roles as saviors if we, as fans, are going to embrace them. Take, for example, Joe Torre. He was an All-Star and MVP in his playing days, but his managerial career got off to kind of a slow start. Then he came to the Yankees before the 1996 season. The press didn't expect much from him, calling him Clueless Joe. But I'm sure Steinbrenner had read him the riot act before he wrote out his first lineup. And then it seemed like the winning would never end; he led the Yankees to the playoffs in each of his twelve seasons at the helm.

Even when the chips were stacked against the Yankees, as the case seemed to be so many times late in the season, with a close pennant race against Boston and the rest of the mighty American League East, then the best-of-five Division Series, and then the American League Championship Series, and then the World Series, Torre was the calming voice of reason. You could just sense his Zen-ness from his pregame chats with the media, sitting in the dugout, slow deep voice, talking for as long as the reporters stuck around to listen. He'd talk about the weather or what it was like to catch Bob Gibson or that time in 1975 when he set the record by grounding into four double plays in a single game. That was part of his wisdom: Keep the media's attention so they don't go messin' with the players. Genius. Tell the media a story; they won't walk away.

By the time Torre was done talking in the dugout, the press had to clear the field, so there was no more time left to interview players. Torre deflected the pressure of the critical media and his meddling boss and in doing so, kept things simple in the clubhouse. It worked because the Yankees always found a way to get to the playoffs. Did I mention Torre is now the manager of the Dodgers? Yeah, I mean, there's pressure out here, we want to win, but he won't have to endure as much scrutiny as he did in New York. He's earned that much.

But anyway. Torre is a native New Yorker. A Brooklynite, like me, I might add. So when the Yankees won the World Series in 1996, the first championship since 1978, the city rallied around its newest favorite son. Let me tell you, there is a lot of pride in New York. And when Torre battled prostate cancer in 1999, all of New York fought with him.

Sure, Torre is a winner because of his record, but he is a hero because he was courageous during challenging times. I'm not suggesting any superlatives here. I'm not saying Torre is the most heroic person in baseball. But a hero must fit into a particular mold, and that is a mold of courageously overcoming obstacles.

Sandy Koufax, a left-handed pitcher for the Dodgers, represents a different kind of hero. Yes, he, too, is from Brooklyn. But that's not why I like him. Okay, maybe that's part of it. And my dad loves him. But that's not why he's a hero. He's a hero simply because he was awesome. Like, Hall of Fame awesome. He played only twelve seasons, which by modern standards is a blink, and he won only 165 games. But his winning percentage is .655, which is the highest among National League pitchers with 2,000 innings since 1913. It's astounding what he accomplished in such a short time.

He was dominant between 1961 and 1966, and he was untouchable in 1963, '65, and '66, winning the pitching Triple Crown (leading the league in wins, strikeouts, and ERA) three times during that span, and throwing four no-hitters, including one perfect game. In 1966, he pitched 323 innings and didn't hit a single batter. He is one of two pitchers since 1946 to win 25 or more games in a season three times. He struck out 2,396 batters in $2,324\frac{1}{3}$ innings, more than one batter per inning.

His final two seasons—'65 and '66—were marked by such intense pain that his entire left arm would be bruised the day after a start, the swelling so bad that his arm could not be straightened. But those were the years he logged more innings ($335\frac{2}{3}$ and 323, respectively) than at any other point in his career. When he retired, he was at the top of his game. But a diagnosis in 1964 of arthritis proved to be insurmountable. He was only thirty years old when he left the game.

If numbers don't make the hero in your book, keep in mind that Koufax was a devout Jew who elected not to pitch Game 1 of the 1965 World Series because it fell on Yom Kippur. Show me a player who's willing to do that today. And if you need a little bit of Koufax pop culture, don't forget he was the subject of an entire episode in *Entourage*'s fourth season on HBO. So, look, the guy's impact was palpable on the field and enduring off of it.

You could say the same thing about Roberto Clemente, the Hall of Fame right fielder for the Pittsburgh Pirates, though his impact off the field can be best described as philanthropic. And philanthropy, in my book, always ranks higher that pop culture. On New Year's Eve in 1972, while on his way to Nicaragua to deliver supplies to earthquake victims, Clemente died in a plane crash.

He played in the bigs for eighteen years, hit a lifetime average of .317 with exactly 3,000 hits, and won twelve Gold Glove Awards and one MVP Award (finishing among the award's top ten finalists seven other times). Additionally, Clemente served in the infantry in the United States Marine Corps Reserves between 1958 and 1964. But when he found out that corrupt government officials intercepted aid intended for the people of Nicaragua, Clemente decided to tag along on the next flight, to ensure that the supplies reached their proper destination. But the plane was overloaded and crashed shortly after takeoff. His body was never recovered.

Clemente was one of the good guys. He didn't use his status as a baseball star to make his life better. The argument could be made, I think, that he would have lived the same philanthropic life had he not been a baseball player, doing his best to make the world a better place, a little more livable.

Of course, none of our baseball heroes, even the apparently saintlike Clemente, are as pure as we hope, and *none* of the bad guys are quite as bad as we imagine. We know now that the deified and beloved Mickey Mantle was a skirt chaser and an alcoholic who would launch some of his legendary home runs hungover. We know now that Roger Maris—long reviled as an aloof, uncaring robot—was so torn up about chasing the single-season home run record that his hair fell out in clumps. Maris's battle against Mantle for Babe Ruth's single-season home run record was the perfect example of how the media play their own role in determining whom we relish and whom we loathe. It wasn't enough that a Yankee was going to break Ruth's record. It had to be the right Yankee, and the right Yankee was Mantle not Maris.

As reporters and baseball historians have revisited that episode, they've revised the original casting of Maris as evildoer, and today he is viewed through the epic lens that he long deserved. Unfortunately, the revisions to history usually don't go that way. Every year seems to hold some new sordid detail about heroes past and present. Joe DiMaggio was a cheapskate. Roger Clemens allegedly used steroids and slept around. Alex Rodriguez is getting divorced.

What's a thinking fan to do? The easy choice is to give in to cynicism. They're all cheats and liars, people can say, and give up on the game altogether. I see that sort of thinking in my business. Once upon a time, people thought actors were as good, and as noble, as the roles they played. Then, with the rise of celebrity journalism and the twenty-four-hour news cycle, indiscretions were publicized, scandals splashed all over newspapers, magazines, and the Internet. And for a lot of people, the truth was obvious: They're all bums! Except they're not. We're not. Ballplayers aren't. No one is.   ·

Not that long ago, I was one of those cynics myself. It was 2000, and I had just returned from three months in South Africa, shooting a miniseries. Just nine years earlier, apartheid had been abolished in that country, and there was change and hope everywhere. I got caught up in the feeling—

the feeling that we could all make a difference, that we could all make the world a better place—and I started volunteering at a children's hospital in a township near where we were shooting. I worked mostly with HIV-positive kids, and the experience changed my life. It helped me realize how much we all have to offer, if we could just forget ourselves and realize we are all part of something larger, that we are all bound by our humanity. It wasn't like any work I had ever done before, and it was gratifying in ways I never could have imagined.

And then the shoot was over and I moved back to Los Angeles. All at once I was thrust back into my life, which only weeks earlier had felt so trivial, and I fell into a deep, deep depression. In South Africa I had been spending time with poor, sick children, trying to ease their burdens, and now I was driving my BMW through the streets of Beverly Hills. I wanted to assimilate the person I had become in that South African hospital with the person I was in Los Angeles. As it turned out, this was much harder than I thought it would be, and when I couldn't immediately shift those gears, it threw me into a tailspin.

It was bad. I'll spare you the gory details but suffice to say that nothing seemed quite right. Activities and friends that I had enjoyed before my trip suddenly felt irrelevant. Because I felt so bad, everything around me looked bad—including (gasp) baseball.

That's right. You heard me. I committed the cardinal sin for a baseball fan: I got a little pessimistic about the game I love. Players I had idolized now had feet of clay in my mind. They weren't stars anymore, merely mercenaries looking for better deals during their contract years; connivers who used illegal drugs to get an edge; and, in some cases, immature idiots cheating on their wives, looking for love, as they say, in all sorts of wrong places.

My attitude toward baseball reflected my attitude toward everything at that time. It was a tough, tough period for me. A guy hit a base-clearing double to win a game? Big deal. He'll probably be holding out for more money next spring. I wonder if he's got a girlfriend near every ballpark. An opposing pitcher looked like he'd been shooting steroids, and was throwing high heat at one of my team's batters. Sigh. So what? Why get worked up? Everyone was probably doing it.

It was summer, I had been a fan for a long time, and not so suddenly, I was wondering how anyone could actually think baseball was pure. I started to see the game through a skeptical filter; it was just a big business, conducted by big businessmen.

In the middle of this unfortunate rut, I moved from Beverly Hills to the country, and that helped a little. I started hiking and spending a lot more time with my pets, and that helped even more. What helped most, though, was figuring out how to bring the joy of the work I did in South Africa into my daily life. I'd always wanted to reach out, but being a celebrity in Los Angeles, there are not a lot of ways to do that other than walking down the red carpet for a cause. Charity events often have a way of creating a natural distance between you and the cause you're supporting. There's nothing wrong with that—there's a lot right with that, in fact—but I wanted something more organic, something more hands-on.

I got in touch with UNICEF, and the organization appointed me a goodwill ambassador and sent me to Angola and India, where I got to meet a lot of children who were in really tough circumstances. But those kids had hope. They *radiated* hope. Visiting those countries made me realize that we're all the same. Humanity is all the same. The only things that separate us are the social and political struggles that happen to be occurring in the territories in which we happen to be born. If we're all the same, then poverty affects us all. Lack of education affects us all. But what binds us is hope. That's the strongest thing that connects us to each other, hope, even—and sometimes especially—when things seem hopeless.

Working with UNICEF (and later, the Global Network for Neglected Tropical Diseases) has helped me keep in mind the necessity of hope, especially to children. Realizing the importance of that hope helped me reconnect with baseball. It helped me lose myself in the game. It allowed me to forget the salary arbitrations and doping rumors and all the other static that seems to surround every human enterprise where there are winners and losers, and to simply root for the home team. Who was I to be moping around? To be cynical? So I stopped.

I hadn't planned to travel halfway around the world to rediscover my love for the game, to appreciate once more the purity of baseball. But luckily for me, not only did I rediscover that love, I emerged a bigger and better fan on the other side. I came to see just how central baseball is to our way of life and to understand why the game—no matter how infected it becomes by the almighty dollar, no matter how it's touched by drugs and sex and all the other things that touch modern life—will always be a child's game with good guys and bad guys. It will always touch the child in all of us, no matter how old.

Sometimes you just need the story of the baseball season to envelop you. This game and its history are built on the backs of these tales that for decades have taken fans away from the things in their lives that they'd rather not think about. The characters, the drama, their actions, are all essential parts of this stagecraft that offers people an escape, if even for a couple of hours, from the aggravations of life. Pulse-pounding flights from certain defeat; heroes who embodied the excesses of the times in which they lived, and triumphed nonetheless; mortals who quietly went about their daily duties until the day they were called upon to do something great, and then delivered what was asked of them. It's all there in baseball, any story line you could possibly desire.

So if a guy hits .350, his heart must be made of gold? If a pitcher's earned run average balloons up to 7.00, he must have spent time with Lucifer plotting the end of the world? A manager calls for a double steal and it works, and he's a genius. It leads to a double play, and he's a moron. It's never that simple, of course. Well, almost never that simple. People are people, and professional athletes are just doing their jobs. They are subject to the same vices of greed, vanity, and arrogance that we all are. But we need them there because we need heroes and we need villains. If we don't have them, we'll simply create them ourselves out of whatever happens to be in front of us.

A lot of players chafe at the roles that fans assign them. "We're not role models," you'll sometimes hear as a player refuses to sign an autograph or talk to a reporter. I see it in my business, too. Actors who take their craft seriously, but have nothing but contempt for the idea that people should emulate them, or look to them for inspiration. I think that's so shortsighted. I think it's such a squandering of a chance to do good.

The truth is, having fans who invest something eventually allows any celebrity—athlete or actor, politician or playwright—to use that investment toward meaningful ends. That's why parents of sick children appreciate it so much when a ballplayer comes to visit. That's what allows me to do my work for UNICEF and the Global Network.

Put eighteen men on a diamond, and give them some gloves and a bat and a ball, and you have a silly game, but we, as fans, have much more. We have a morality tale, an epic, mythic struggle. We have something to take our minds off our complicated, nuanced, and compromised lives. We have a spectacle. We have archetypes of good and . . . if not evil, certainly, bad.

Now you might be thinking to yourself, Good? Evil? Is that stretching it a bit?

No. It most certainly is not.

That's the way it's always been, and I'm not just talking about the days of Pee Wee Reese and Lou Gehrig. I'm talking about ancient Greece, when Hercules fought the fearsome

Cerberus of the Underworld (and kicked his ass, I might add). I'm talking about old-time Norway, where that god Thor slugged it out with Jörmungand. I'm talking about Superman versus Lex Luthor, Spiderman versus Doctor Octopus. Mortals scrapping over a few bucks, or a corner office, might be diverting, but it's not what we need. We need something larger than us. We need heroic battles. We need heroes.

I'm not the only one who's made that discovery. In the autumn of 2001, after the horrors of 9/11, when an entire country was grieving and in shock, the New York Yankees, with their ninth-inning home runs and improbable come-from-behind victories and enormous grit, gave hope to an entire country. Sure, they were just baseball players and we were just fans, but for a moment we were all joined in something that collectively was larger than any of us as individuals. And that was a moment when we most needed to be joined together. That was a moment when we most needed baseball.

chapter four

(Baseball x Age)– Playoff Appearances = Life

Life will always throw you curves; just keep fouling them off. The right pitch will come, but when it does be prepared to run the bases.
—RICK MAKSIAN

*I*t's about time I attempt to address a cliché that has been floating around this game for a good 150 years: Baseball is like life.

If you've been a fan for a while you've no doubt heard some version of this idea uttered before. If you're newer to the game, trust me, you'll hear this again. The annals of baseball writing are littered with books, columns, leaflets, placards, postcards, and notes passed around fifth-grade classrooms from just about every era, all of which talk about the myriad of reasons why baseball is like life. Sportswriters and fans alike have long found just about every reason there is to draw the comparison between life and baseball. With varying degrees of romantic prose and detailed analogies, baseball, they say, carries with it all the hallmarks, hardships, and triumphs that we face in our everyday lives as Americans. Some of these reasons are more compelling than others, but all come from a place of wanting desperately to believe that the rules that govern our national pastime can somehow also apply to our daily routines.

Clichés are clichés for a reason, and often something doesn't become a cliché unless it's rooted in some measure of fact. And yet over the last couple of seasons, I found myself questioning this supposed truism of baseball romanticism. I found myself really asking the question: Is baseball like life?

Okay, okay, before you throw this book across the room in anger because I'm even *questioning* this concept, just hear me out. I'll start by saying that no one wants baseball to be just like life more than I do. To see the game as that perfect mirror, our world reflected in a simple series of nine innings on the field, is an incredibly appealing thought— perhaps that's why it's been around for so long.

It's even more appealing when you think about how *not* like life the other professional sports are. Football has its charms: the swift and cagey running backs; the quarterbacks admired for their rubbery arms but revered for their uncanny split-second decision-making skills; the predatory linebackers; the lineman, anonymous and doughty and indomitable. But football is not like life. Football is, to paraphrase the late George Carlin, like a military campaign. Blitzes and bombs, attacks and last stands. There is a satisfying finality to it all, except when there isn't. Then there's overtime. And even when that's done, there are arguments. What if that team hadn't won the coin toss? What if the field hadn't been so muddy? Football is strategic and thrilling and fun to watch, but it's not like life.

I like basketball, too, with its overt athleticism and liquid action, its ever-shifting combinations of physical artistry and snarling strength, its lobs and back-door screens and the way that individual stars, no matter how brightly they burn, eventually find ways to nestle snugly into the team firmament . . . or they simply burn out. But if football inclines toward the military, toward the attack and counterattack, then basketball resembles modern dance. Basketball is constant action and poetry and interpretation. It's beautiful and inspiring, simple and complex at the same time, but it's not like life either.

Is *baseball* like life, though? I started to ponder this not out of frustration with the game or being fed up with the Dodgers, but simply because the truism is invoked so often. It's one of those cards that journalists play throughout the season until you simply accept it, and so for a long time I did.

Frequently it's during the moments of highest tension and drama that people are prone to stating that baseball is like life. Take for instance Ozzie Smith in 1985, in the fifth game of the National League Championship Series against the Dodgers. Smith, a .276 hitter that season, was up in the ninth inning, facing Tom Niedenfuer. Beloved and admired for the way he had redefined his position, Smith was the consummate team player, utterly devoid of significant power. He had hit 13 home runs—all from the right side—since his rookie season in 1978. He would bunt. He would make Dwight Gooden throw a lot of pitches. He would somehow get on base, give brutes like George Hendrick and Jack Clark a chance to win the game. That's what they did—win games with their bat. Smith would do what he did, and let the power hitters do what they did.

Except that's not what happened. With a 1–2 count, the five-eleven, 150-pound Smith, batting left-handed, launched a line drive to the right-field corner. For an instant, there was an odd, otherwordly hush—imagine a sound if you saw something that made no sense at all, but that was all the more glorious for its utter lack of sense—and then, a magnificent din.

"Go crazy, folks!" the Cardinals announcer, Jack Buck, shouted into his microphone. For generations of Cardinals fans, Buck had played his role too. His was the quiet, dignified, restrained voice of baseball, the man who delivered witty and dry commentary that made most announcers sound like overenthusiastic hicks. But now Buck was doing something he didn't do either. Fate had also tapped Buck on the shoulder. "Go crazy, folks!" he shouted again. And again.

Wild Pitch Life (and Death) with the Game

The Yankees have had three players die in plane crashes, none arguably more shocking than when Thurman Munson, the team's first captain since Lou Gehrig, died in 1979.

Munson was a family man, and life on the road was often too much for him to take. He eventually learned how to fly so that after games, he could fly out of the Teterboro airport in New Jersey and be home in Ohio faster than he could fight New York traffic on his way to his empty apartment.

On August 2, 1979, Munson's Cessna jet came up short of the runway and burst into flames when it hit the ground in Canton, Ohio. Though his two companions were able to escape the fire, Munson was trapped and died. He was thirty-two years old.

The news stunned everyone, much like the news of the death of Roberto Clemente, who also died in a plane crash. The Yankees immediately retired Munson's number 15 and his locker. To this day, no one has ever taken residence in the far corner slot in the Yankees clubhouse.

On March 9, 1991, former Yankees pitcher Jim

Hardin died when the propeller on his Beech airplane failed to respond shortly after takeoff. Hardin was forced to return and attempt an emergency landing. During the plane's descent, Hardin was able to steer away from a Little League ballfield with children playing on it. His plane crashed, killing him, in the parking lot of a T.G.I. Friday's that was still under construction. He was forty-seven.

Then, on October 11, 2006, Yankees pitcher Cory Lidle and his twenty-six-year-old flight instructor died when Lidle's small Cirrus airplane crashed into a high-rise apartment complex at York Avenue and East Seventy-second Street on Manhattan's Upper East Side. Like Munson, Lidle found solitude in the open skies, and before he was to fly west for the off-season, Lidle wanted to take one last look at Manhattan. He circled the Statue of Liberty before heading up the East River, taking in Brooklyn and Queens to the right and Manhattan to the left. He lost radio contact around the Fifty-ninth Street Bridge and crashed into the Belaire Apartments after attempting to make a U-turn. He was thirty-four.

★

And let me put this on the table: Kirk Gibson's walk-off homer in Game 1 of the 1988 World Series between the Dodgers and Athletics is the best ever. Period. Okay, maybe overstated. But Gibson, the '88 NL MVP, wasn't expected to play at all in the World Series after injuring both of his legs in the NLCS, not to mention suffering from a stomach virus at the start of Game 1. Indeed, Gibson got only one at bat during the World Series, and he made it count.

It's a scenario we've all imitated at one point or another. Two out. Bottom of the ninth. Runner on first. Down by two. Star player comes to the plate. Limping. He's hurt. The last hope. Count quickly goes 0–2. Works it, 3–2. Batter steps out. Breath. Pause. Pitch. Swing. And Vin takes it from there:

High fly ball to right field . . . She is . . . GONE!

I still get goose bumps seeing the replay. Gibson limp-walking around the bases, pumping his arms like he's starting a lawn mower. Dodgers win by one. Fucking awesome. Gibson's home run is probably the most dramatic moment in my personal baseball history.

Nevertheless, when I thought about defining, high-tension stories like Gibson's or Smith's home run, I found it hard to see the parallels to life outside the game. Hear me out: Walk-off home runs make anyone love baseball. They're final, and they're melodramatic, and they're resonant. They're single instances of heroism against long odds. They tell stories of one player who had the chance to do something memorable and seized that chance. For all these reasons and more, walk-off home runs may be the crowning achievement in a sport loaded with them—the epitome of the drama and the tension that comes with a good game.

Pity the fan who sees a walk-off homer the first time she visits a ballpark. It's like the woman who throws a line into a lake and pulls out a thirty-pound catfish, or a man in the mountains who decides he'll sift some river silt through his fingers, and discovers a nugget of gold. Those are folks who have glimpsed glory on their first effort, and might suspect that things are always that glorious. Walk-off home runs awaken everything that's human in us, or at least everything that believes in fairy tales. Think about it. Your tribe, or your family, or your country, is about to suffer a terrible loss. Their last hope is you. Fail, and your people are vanquished. Succeed, and they triumph. But there is another one—actually, another nine—who are dedicated to beating your tribe and to making sure you fail. Then you deliver. The walk-off homer is the Little Engine That Could. It's the turtle who kicks the rabbit's speedy ass. It's Sleeping Beauty and Cinderella and Hansel and Gretel getting away from the cannibal witch and Ali coming off the ropes to shake off age and doubt and fear and to reclaim his championship. It's every other happy ending in the face of long odds you've ever heard of.

Those who err on the side of romanticism like to cite walk-off home runs like Ozzie's or Gibson's as prime examples of how baseball is like life. On the one hand, it makes sense to think this way—after all, who wouldn't like to believe that the game's most dramatic moments are what make it just like our everyday lives? On the other hand, this drama is precisely the problem. How many people do you know who have lives with a Cinderella ending?

As I explored this contradiction, I found myself looking back on my life and wondering when the last time was that my workday or my month was hanging in the balance of one lone plate appearance? Sure, there were plenty of times that I felt pressure to succeed, times when I needed to bring my A game to whatever I was doing, but I had no bottom-of-the-ninth moments. I might always swing for the fences, but that doesn't make me Mickey Mantle.

For most people (myself included), our lives are a series of quiet decisions that have a profound impact. I'd love to live in a world where there was an equivalent to a walk-off home run opportunity all the time, but that's life as I imagine it, not as it actually is. Walk-off home runs are fairy tales; they're baseball's version of happily ever after. And life, as I'm sure your mother, father, or ninth-grade science teacher probably told you, is not like a fairy tale. We don't defeat the other team with one swing of the bat and then ride the bases into the sunset.

The more I turned over these ideas about baseball and life in my head, the more I found that what makes the cliché true is not the walk-off home runs or the singular moments of glory. It's what happens after those moments—the moments of humanity and humility that arrive after the walk-off home runs and bottom-of-the-ninth strikeouts. Take Mark "the Bird" Fidrych. Tall, gangly, curly-haired, he talked to baseballs. He manicured the mound in between pitches. He sent back balls to the umpire, saying "they had hits in them." He wore tight blue jeans and drove a green subcompact, and in 1976, if you were a fan and if you still had a little of the rebel in you, then the Bird would have been a star.

In his very first appearance, the Bird pitched a complete game, gave up only two hits, and led the Detroit Tigers to victory. And it got better. He had 19 victories his first year, started in the All-Star Game, and while he was at it, was on the cover of *Rolling Stone* (the first athlete ever to have that honor). Had there ever been a baseball pitcher like Fidrych, an athlete better suited to his age? Ironic, individualistic, a me-driven hurler mowing down batters in the Me Decade? Actually, there had been and there would be.

Here's the thing about the Bird: He had a great rookie year, and that was about it. The Bird's career ended after five short seasons due to an undiagnosed rotator cuff injury. Now he owns a farm. Ozzie Smith is retired. So is Kirk Gibson. They may have achieved greatness, but now they're normal people, living their lives away from the game. The truth is, all the role players—no matter how gritty and glorious, no matter how mighty and magisterial—hang up their cleats when the game is done, and then they go home to the rest of their lives. Sadly, for every walk-off home run, there are scores of final outs.

Stories like the Bird's remind us how in baseball, like in life, we have to take the bad with the good; we don't have the ability to pick and choose the moments that we acknowledge. We don't get to decide which bills to pay and which to ignore. We have to face them all, and the same is true for baseball. The game doesn't allow us to remember just the home runs or the bases-loaded singles. Fans have no choice but to recall the instances when we watched failure creep up and pull the ground out from under us (something Cubs fans know all too well).

Baseball, like life, is as much about missed chances and ignominious endings as it is about singles and doubles. It's about spring phemons and late-season burnouts. It's about players like Babe Ruth, whom everyone reveres, and players like Bill Buckner, who has become the definition of the word "scapegoat." Buckner, a solid veteran with a solid career and terrible knees, was brought in late in Game 6 of the 1986 World Series between the Red Sox and Mets. Boston led the series 3–2 and held a two-run lead with two outs in the bottom of the tenth inning at Shea. The Mets came back and tied it, thanks to three singles and a wild pitch. But it looked like the damage was over when Mookie Wilson nubbed a grounder to Buckner at first base, an easy out. Not so. The ball rolled between Buckner's legs and into right field, allowing Ray Knight to score the winning run. The Mets forced Game 7, which they won, and captured their first World Series since 1969.

It's unfortunate, really, because looking at the numbers, Buckner was a fine fielder. In 1,555 games as a first baseman, Buckner made only 128 errors. While that number might seem high, keep in mind that the ball is thrown to first more than to any other bag. Think of the number of times he had fielded balls like that. How often, in practice and in the game, he put his glove down to the dirt and felt the ball roll inside. And yet somehow, this one time, he missed it. If only, Mr. Buckner, if only.

Every team has its own Bill Buckner stories—instances when the fairy tale turns against us, when the pop outs, strikeouts, and ground outs don't fit our happily ever after.

Blown saves. Missed opportunities. Routine ground balls booted. Wild pitches. Slumps. Control problems. The mighty slugger who has a chance to take immortality by the throat and to shake it, to establish his role among the game's heroes . . . and, then, like Mighty Casey at the Bat, whiffs. Life is, all too often, no joy, no joy at all, in Mudville.

It's that full tapestry of memory that makes this game like life. Knowing what happened the season *after* your team won it all, the season when the owners sold away all your good players, leaving the team decimated and in last place. Knowing what happened when your aging slugger decided to stave off retirement for one more year, only to encounter a dismal season that tarnished his bright memory just a touch. Baseball doesn't allow us to be selective with our memories, just as in life we can't simply delete the parts of our past that we don't care to remember. Sooner or later it all catches up with you.

This is something I encounter in Hollywood as well. Hollywood is subject to its own clichés of glamour and gloss, and while those are certainly rooted in truth, the reality is more complicated. Buried beneath the walk-off home runs of Hollywood (let's say the Oscars), the competition is fierce and backbreaking. You have to contend with some people who intend to succeed no matter what the price. You have to face the constant influx of new people coming up through the ranks who are younger and perhaps more talented. It's a cycle that creates a me-first attitude, and instills insecurity in just about everyone. That's why for every success you hear about in Hollywood there are scores of failures. It's a place that tears down dreams a lot more than it makes them.

The only way to combat that culture is to be yourself, work hard, and do your best. To show up, perform every day like it is your last, and know why you're doing it in the first place. Personally, I work to make a living. I work to be able to give back and have a voice to effect change. I work because though I love my job, at the end of the day, it is only a job.

In the end my motivations aren't that different from what gets most people to the office every morning or gets ball-players to the park every day. Life for me is about getting up and going to work, about putting myself out there and having people tell me thanks but no thanks. It's about trying and failing, and trying and failing, and trying and failing some more, until you don't fail, until bliss descends upon those who have not given up.

Life is like baseball not because of the majesty of the walk-off home run or the beauty of the perfect game, but because life and baseball are both about the roles that we play every day, the roles that we fulfill whether we like them or not. In life and on any given day, you might be a daughter, a sister, a producer, and/or a girlfriend. You might have to do any number of things to fulfill your obligations not because your season hangs in the balance, but because it's the role that's been prescribed for you.

Likewise a shortstop needs to have a strong arm and good reflexes until he's leading off the sixth inning in a tied game. Then he needs to possess a quick bat and opposite-field power. Unless his manager asks him to bunt, in which case he'd better have soft hands and a good eye. The slugger needs to slug. It's what he's there to do, but when his team needs him to take a few pitches to tire out the opposing pitcher, he needs to fulfill that commitment as well.

The roles may not always be glamorous, but they are essential. They are the roles that we need to play to make it through life. They may not let us always swing away, but they get us through nine innings and then some. They exist in baseball, and they exist in everyday life, too.

In the end, this baseball truism does hold up. There are more than a few reasons why baseball is like life. But perhaps the most resonant connection is one that I haven't mentioned yet. Perhaps the real connection between these two is that both allow us to keep dreaming. Both give us the faith that we need to keep going. The faith that makes us fans yearn for Babe Ruth and forget about Mighty Casey. The faith that helps us wake up in the morning. The faith that leads you to yearn for Ozzie and Kirk, believe in spring phenoms, hope against hope that magic and mystery will descend from the sky above your team, like lightning on a summer night. The faith that forces you to see the positive when all others can see is hopelessness. It's the faith of a fan, but it's also the faith of a human.

You can't help but see that kind of faith in this simple game of nine innings, or for that matter in life, too.

chapter *five*

The Numbers

No matter how good you are, you're going to lose
one-third of your games. No matter how bad you
are, you are going to win one-third of your games.
It's the other third that makes the difference.

—TOMMY LASORDA

aseball is a game of singular achievement mixed in with a lot of disappointment. The former almost always follows a whole lot of the latter. Ground out, strike out, single, pop up, single, strike out, ground into a double play, home run. In a lot of professions, that kind of failure rate guarantees you a lifetime spot in lower middle management, or worse. In baseball, come through one out of three times and you're in the Hall of Fame.

How can it be? That's what I wondered when I first started watching games. As just about any new baseball fan can attest, when you first get into the game, there's a lot of confusion over all the numbers that people throw out. Some of it's terminology, but much of it is simply understanding the relatively small differences between numbers that are considered good and numbers that are considered bad.

As a young girl trying to understand the game, I asked just about everyone to explain it all to me. Not only did I not know what all the numbers were, I was still trying to learn what numbers in general meant. The years went by and my math skills caught up with my fandom, but still there were always lingering questions about why all these figures actually mattered.

I asked my father, my brother, and anyone else who might help me appreciate these subtleties. And that's how I came to really learn The Numbers (I use capitalization when it comes to The Numbers because they are such an integral part of the game that they might as well be a player).

Learning about The Numbers of the game can be a daunting task. When I first became a fan, what got me excited about them was the simple notion that The Numbers offered a pretty good indication of where a player's career would end up. They gave me a sense of whether I was watching history in the making or just another slugger having a solid year. Was I cheering for a future Hall of Famer or simply a player who was playing up in a contract year?

And that was just the front door that The Numbers

opened. In addition, I started to find that The Numbers offered me insight into the character of the players that were on my team's roster. They helped highlight the differences between the players who were clutch and those who cracked under the pressure. I came to see that it was one thing for my marquee player to bat above .300 for a season, but if he was batting only .250 with runners in scoring position, he really couldn't be that great of a star. Similarly, if there was a Dodger who could never muster the power to hit more than 10 home runs a season, but always managed to hit an extra-base hit with a runner on first, could he really be that weak at the plate?

Suddenly I began to ask myself questions about how we as fans value the players on our teams and how we decide who our favorites are. The Numbers laid bare all the facts. What good is a $15-million-a-year player if his resolve fails him with two on, no out in the bottom of the ninth? How bad can a player really be if he can produce when his team needs him the most? In that sense, The Numbers gave me another way to evaluate what it really meant to be good in this game. They had the ability to show me who was sweating it in crucial situations and who was cool as a cucumber.

No one studies them harder, pores over them more fiercely, or trusts them more ferociously than a certain kind of hard-core baseball fan. How hard-core? A twenty-nine-year-old outfielder named Ryan Ludwick, after bouncing around the minor leagues for almost nine years, got a shot with the St. Louis Cardinals in 2007. He responded with a slugging percentage (total bases divided by at bats) of .479 in 300 at bats, and got a starting role in 2008. At the end of August 2008, he was hitting .309 (eighth in the National League), with 31 home runs (second), and 95 RBIs (fourth). The more credulous and naive saw another Stan Musial or Lou Brock. But the forecasting system used by Baseball Prospectus projected—based on equations factoring in Ludwick's past performance, his age, and other data that would give even a mathematics professor headaches—that next season, Ludwick's on-base percentage would lose 27 points and his slugging percentage 81 points.

Cold? I think so. But usually true. And while not important for the casual fan, The Numbers are absolutely critical if you want to *really* appreciate just how subtle this game really is. That's because The Numbers not only help you see how truly rare real excellence is, but help you predict it, and analyze it, and spend all your idle hours thinking about situations where it might occur.

Take batting averages. In simpler times, you divided the number of hits a player got by the number of at bats, and voilà, you had a number. Or the earned run average. Simply put, ERA is the number of earned runs a pitcher gives up per nine innings. To get that number, multiply the total number of earned runs by nine. Divide that number by the total innings pitched, and there you go. So in 1961, when Whitey Ford won the Cy Young, he gave up 101 earned runs, multiplied by nine is 909, divided by 283 innings, and you get 3.21, a top-ten average in 1961.

Other critical numbers include on-base percentage and walks plus hits per innings pitched, or WHIP (see the glossary for a better explanation of this). Keep Bobby Abreu in mind when you talk about on-base percentage. Abreu's lifetime batting average of .300 doesn't tell the whole story. As the saying goes, a walk is as good as a hit, and Abreu perennially leads the league in bases on balls and receives his fair share of free passes via the hit-by-pitch.

As an example, let's work with Abreu's numbers from 2005, his strong final full season with the Phillies. Combine hits (168) with walks (117) and the number of times he was hit by the pitch (6); that number is 291, representing the number of times in 2005 that Abreu safely reached base, not by an error or fielder's choice. Next, add at bats (588), walks (117), times he was hit by the pitch (6), and sacrifices for a total of 719 plate appearances. Now, stay with me, we're almost done. Divide the number of times Abreu reached base safely (291) by his total plate appearances (719), and what you have is his on-base percentage, .40472. Round it up to .405, and Abreu was seventh in the NL in on-base percentage, a real offensive threat.

Calculating WHIP, an indication of how many base runners a pitcher allows per inning, is less complicated. Divide the number of hits plus walks a pitcher has allowed by innings pitched. Let's look at Koufax's 1966 season as an example. He gave up 241 hits and walked 77 batters for a total of 318 base runners. Divide 318 by 323 innings pitched, and his WHIP was .985, which ranked second in the NL that year.

But those were simpler times. Today, there are stats for *everything*. Batting average with runners on base. Strikeouts against left-handed batters. ERA against rookies whose last name ends with a G, in night games, when the moon is in its fourth phase.

Okay, the last is a joke (I think), but barely.

Wild Pitch Location, Location, Location . . .

People say baseball is a game of inches. I'd add that it's where those inches are measured that matters, too. Take two infamous instances of fan misbehavior. One of the fans became a local hero; the other was virtually run out of town. Let's take the poor Chicagoan first. . . .

The scene: National League Championship Series (NLCS) Game 6; Cubs leading the series, 3–2, against the Marlins; Wrigley Field; Mark Prior, the once and never dominant starter he was tabbed to be, is uninjured and *actually* on the mound, pitching a three-hit shutout for the Cubbies with one out in the eighth inning. The Cubs haven't been to the World Series since 1945 and haven't won it since 1908. Steve Bartman—from Northbrook, Illinois, a Notre Dame grad and Cubs enthusiast since birth, even traveling to Arizona to watch spring training—eyes the action from the first row along the left-field foul line, behind the bullpen.

Crack! High fly ball, drifting foul, off the bat of Luis Castillo. Juan Pierre pauses off second base to get a read, but it's going out of play. Cubs left fielder Moises Alou comes in to make the grab, but wait! As Alou reaches, he knocks into Bartman, who, reaching out his glove to make the grab, has been following the ball and not the fielder. He never saw Alou coming for the catch. Alou drops the ball!

Ugh, there could have been two out. But no, Castillo drew a walk, and on ball four, Prior threw a wild pitch, allowing Pierre to take third. Ivan Rodriguez singled, driving in Pierre, the score was now 3–1 with one out, and the Marlins were on their way to an eight-run inning, making way for the final 8–3 win.

The next night, the Marlins beat Kerry Wood and won the series. Then they beat the Yankees in the World Series.

Whom do you think Cubs fans, crazy as they are, blamed for the NLCS loss? Steve Bartman had to be led away under police escort for his own safety. Even as he walked out under the police officers' guidance, fans lobbed trash, beer cups, and insults his way. Cubs players and personnel absolved Bartman in public statements, but the fans wouldn't have any of it. Bartman's family had to change their phone numbers, and he never relished his newly public life. He declined interviews. He requested that Marlins fans who sent him gifts redirect their donations to the Juvenile Diabetes Research Foundation. And when he was offered $25,000 to autograph a photo of the infamous moment of impact with Alou, he refused.

What would have happened had Bartman's grab helped his home team? For the answer to that, let's turn our eyes to the Big Apple, and little Jeffrey Maier. In Game 1 of the 1996 American League Championship Series against the Baltimore Orioles, Maier became a part of Yankee Stadium's great tapestry. The Yankees were down, 4–3, in the home half of the eighth when Derek Jeter stepped up to the plate and hit a fly ball to deep right field. Tony Tarasco drifted back, back, back, leaped to make the grab, but wait! It was snagged by a twelve-year-old boy! That little boy was Maier, and at that moment, a new star was born.

Despite the Orioles' accurate protests of fan interference, the home run counted, the score was tied, and the Yankees won the game in the bottom of the eleventh with a Bernie Williams homer. The Yankees won the series, 4–1, and beat the San Diego Padres in the World Series in six games.

Maier entered those awkward teenager years as a footnote to all of this and had a successful career as a college player. Supposedly, he's currently looking for a front-office job in Major League Baseball. The Yankees, well, they installed a pole along the outfield concourse to discourage fans from reaching more potential home run balls.

Maier's catch changed the outcome of the game, which impacted the series, which begot a World Series win, their first since 1978.

★

When did baseball become so numeral-drenched, so stats-obsessed? It's always been so, and that's one explanation for its charm. Anyone with a newspaper or a computer screen can look at a box score and envision action, can see heroism. Basketball box scores might tell you that a player shot 15-for-24, but you don't know when the shots went in, or in what situations. Baseball is different. Numbers are a sportswriter's best friend, but they can also render him useless. Study a scorecard, and you can almost see an entire game. Break the game down further, and you can study every pitch. Break the game down further, analyze every single pitch that's ever been thrown, every swing swung, every ground ball picked up or missed, every fly ball, and you are in a surreal landscape of fractions and integers, statistical models and predictive calculus. You are in Bill James land.

Bill James is a baseball statistician. Beginning in 1977, James annually self-published *The Bill James Baseball Abstract*, in which he pored over stats and box scores and offered up analyses based on the previous season's numbers.

James is credited with coming up with stats to adjust for the differences in ballparks, as well as creating the Pythagorean winning percentage and the power/speed number system (as in Jose Canseco being the first 40/40 player, hitting 40 home runs and stealing 40 bases in the same season).

A lot of teams bought into his concepts, including the Oakland A's, as chronicled in the 2003 Michael Lewis book *Moneyball*. General manager Billy Beane had a tight budget, so he tried to get the most bang for his buck by acquiring players who had great numbers in stats that actually mattered. What difference does it make, he must have thought, if Player X is hitting .350, but only .210 with runners in scoring position? So he went out and got the players who were far from marquee types but who hit with runners on second and third. James is currently a special adviser for the Red Sox.

I'm as big a believer in the Jamesian era as the next gal, and there's no disputing the wisdom of The Numbers. I mean, a guy who's 1-for-30 the past ten games with runners in scoring position is almost certainly not going to deliver in the clutch tomorrow.

But here's the thing that I love about The Numbers: Sometimes, they're wrong. Sometimes he does deliver. For all the computer models and statistical analysis, baseball is still a game of flesh and blood. For all the permutations and combinations that you can work out in your head, there are no absolutes in baseball. Ever. It doesn't matter who's doing the math. That's the beauty of the sport and what makes any game worth watching. That's why you still get excited even when a guy who's 0 for his last 20 at bats comes to the plate against a starter with a 1.69 ERA with a runner on third in the fourth inning: because it has to end sometime. Maybe this will be the first hit in twenty at bats, and maybe he'll go twenty more at bats before getting another, but he still could come through.

The Numbers give me something tangible to ride my hopes on, a feeling to anticipate. If my team is down by two in the bottom of the ninth, the bases are loaded with two outs, and someone comes up to the plate who has hit four grand slams in his career, I know the great walk-off grand slam is at least a possibility. If someone comes up to the plate in the same situation who is batting below the Mendoza line with men on base, it is pretty safe to say, you can pack up your things. That's not to say that the game isn't full of surprises. Sometimes the guy batting below the Mendoza line can win the game for you, sure. And if he does, the moment is even more spectacular, adding to the thrill of it all.

So when the slumping ballplayer is walking to the plate, you'll sit there in your living room with a couple of friends and your brother, and you'll say something along the lines of "He's going to break out with this at bat." A hush will fall over everyone in the room before they burst out laughing and look at you like you just said Jose Canseco would be leading the next baseball commission on performance-enhancing drugs. Then on the third pitch, with the count 1–1, the batter will hit a fast-moving dribbler toward short. The shortstop will dive for it and just barely miss, and the ball will roll ever so slowly into left field. The runner on third will score and the streak will be broken. At least for today.

Not that this has ever happened to me. . .

You can shake the Magic 8-Ball all you want, but in the end, "All Signs Point to Yes" still doesn't give you a definitive answer. Anyone with a computer and a set of stats could have told you that sending Kirk Gibson up to face Dennis Eckersley in the ninth inning, with Gibson's legs barely functional, didn't make sense. But Tommy Lasorda did it anyway.

As the guy who basically invented nuclear physics once famously remarked, "Imagination is more important than knowledge. Knowledge is limited. Imagination encircles the world." Say what you want about the theory of relativity. I say Albert Einstein would have made a hell of a manager.

chapter six

Baseball Finds You When You Need It Most

*Chance is always powerful. Let your hook be
always cast; in the pool where you least expect it,
there will be a fish.*

—OVID

Baseball finds you when you need it most. That's a sentiment that might strike a lot of people as odd. How can a game find anyone? How can a sport tell who needs it? How can a pastime satisfy longing, or soothe disappointment, or lift a person's eyes from her personal disappointments and allow her to see the joy and the light all around her? How can a sport save someone?

If you're a fan, if you've been saved, you know the answers, even if talk of salvation through no-hitters embarrasses you, even if your only evidence of baseball's transcendent power is a yellowing, dusty scorecard you keep in your basement or the lucky cap you wear on days your team plays. If you're not a fan, you might suspect that anyone who invests his hopes and dreams in an athletic sideshow is someone who needs to get out more.

I don't pretend to speak for all fans, and I don't flatter myself that my love affair with baseball is going to convince anyone else to love it too. All I can tell you is how—without my seeking it, and without my knowing how much I needed it—the game found me when I needed it most.

I was in my twenties, and like a lot of women and men in their twenties, I was doing my best to navigate that place between adolescence and adulthood. I had achieved some success as an actress. I had boyfriends, and enough money, and a family that loved me. And, like other people that age, I felt lost.

Those of you who have been in your twenties know what I'm talking about. Those of you who are about to be in your twenties can imagine what I'm talking about. Those of you who are in your twenties now *definitely* know what I'm talking about. Some people assume that if you work in Hollywood, you must be immune to the kind of existential questioning that troubles most people in their twenties. They assume that you must be so happy with your job that you don't ask questions like What am I supposed to do here? What have I been doing with my life? Am I really going anywhere? Do I really want a veggie burrito for dinner? (Yes, that is an existential question for some of us.)

The truth is that if anything, being in Hollywood makes you more prone to these sorts of big-picture questions. The entertainment industry is all about motion. What are you doing next? What's your next move, your next deal? It's very easy to spend several years wrapped up in these specifics, only to find yourself on the other side of all those decisions, and not totally sure how you got there. You'd better believe that in a place where entire careers are based on something as fleeting as physical appearance, there are a lot of people who sit around trying to figure out what they were really meant to do.

And that's precisely what I was doing when baseball found me.

I wish I could tell you that I heard a voice in a dream, à la *Field of Dreams*, saying something along the lines of "If you build it, he will come." Maybe something like "Go to Dodger Stadium, and you will find yourself." I wish I could tell you that my father, who introduced me to the game when I was a child, called me into his oak-paneled study one night, offered me a snifter of brandy, and said, "Alyssa Jayne Milano, I've been thinking, and I've decided that the time is right to introduce you to the world of the hit-and-run and the off-speed curve, to tutor you in the fathomless knowledge of hitting streaks and slugging percentages. I think it is time you put childish things aside and became an adult."

But I can't tell you that, and not just because my dad doesn't have an oak-paneled study, or because he probably thinks snifters are a breed of odd California poodle. The truth is, my dad never talked to me like that (does any father talk to his daughter like that?). What happened was this: I was sitting in my kitchen one night reading a magazine when my mom called and asked what I was doing. I told her nothing, which was basically true, and she told me that Dad was watching a ball game, and why didn't I come over and keep him company.

I don't remember whom the Dodgers were playing that night, or whether my dad talked more about the wonders of Brooklyn. (I'm pretty sure that he talked about Brooklyn, since there are very few days that go by when he does not utter something about Brooklyn.) And I remember that I had a Diet Coke and at one point my mom came into the living room, gave us each a plate of baked ziti, and said, "Isn't this nice, honey?" without addressing either one of us directly. I still wonder whom she was talking to.

Some people stumble on magic in the most unlikely places, and don't even realize it until years later, when their lives are surrounded by magic. I know a guy who went through a terrible breakup with his girlfriend, and was a junior in college, living in Ann Arbor, spending a lot of his afternoons in his dorm room, staring at the ceiling, playing the song he and his girlfriend had listened to, over and over and over again, until his roommate couldn't stand it anymore.

"C'mon, dude," his roommate said, "we're going to a ball game."

So they went to see the Tigers play in Detroit, at Tiger Stadium. It was 2000, and the Tigers hadn't won a World Championship since 1968 (they had losing seasons from 1994 to 2005). But his roommate insisted (wouldn't anyone, after being forced to hear "Who Let the Dogs Out" a thousand times?) So they took in a game. He ended up becoming a fan. He ended up starting to forget about his girlfriend. Today? He's married (to a different woman). He doesn't listen to "Who Let the Dogs Out" anymore (thankfully). And he never misses a Tigers game on television or the radio.

I know another person, a business executive, a friend of a friend's father, who was widowed at sixty-three. He grieved, of course, as anyone would, and he put a lot of his grief into his work, and he spent time with friends, and eventually he even went on a few dates. And then one day a business associate invited him to a game at Miller Park. It was midsummer, and the Milwaukee Brewers were nowhere near the top of their division. In many ways it was a meaningless game, in an ordinary season. But for some reason, it was an important game to this man. Something about the game—was it the manager's tendency to call for double steals and hit-and-runs when other managers would play it cautious? was it the way the team's slugger struck out twice, but kept swinging away until he blasted a late-inning homer?—connected with the widower. He's in his seventies now, remarried and retired. And he's a fan.

Me? Well it all began (again) for me that night with my father and the Dodgers. It wasn't so much that I had ever stopped being a fan, but I had become a pretty distracted one. Life had pulled me away, and it was hard to find balance. I was working seventy-hour weeks and trying to maintain friendships, all while attempting to figure out who I was and what I believed in. I was trying to make time for my family—not to mention there was the whole love/relationship/dating thing. It seemed there just wasn't enough room in my life to be a fanatic when everything else at that time felt more relevant and important to my daily existence. I didn't go to games much and rarely watched them on TV. I followed what was happening, but I didn't pay nearly as much attention as I once had.

But then somehow it all changed watching the Dodgers that night. It started a kind of ritual: a couple nights a week, I would drive over and watch the game, or, because this was in a time before every game was televised, we'd listen to it on the radio. We'd sit together, and I'd have my soda, and my mom would bring something to eat, and my dad and I would be Dodger fans together.

Those were good nights, but they were tough years. Maybe, now that I think about it, the nights were so good because the years were so tough. I was trying make a place for myself in the world, just like lots of other people in their twenties, and just like lots of them, it would have been easy to lose my way. Especially in a place like Los Angeles, in a profession like mine, where you're always beautiful, babe, and wonderful, and a *star,* and yeah, we love you, we absolutely love you, you're the best, the role is definitely yours, until they don't, and you're not, and it's not, either, and don't call us, we'll call you.

I went through my share of rejection and character-building work. I wondered if this career path was the right one for me or if I would find more fulfillment doing something else. I got married and divorced. I often felt overwhelmed. I struggled to find perspective. Maybe I would have turned out just fine without those nights at my parents' house, but I'm glad I didn't have to find out.

Those nights gave me an escape that was unlike anything else that I had in my life at that point. Instead of thinking about acting, I could listen to Vin and get lost in the drama of a 3–2 count. Instead of pondering what I was supposed to be doing with my life, I was laughing about a passing remark that my dad made after a very, very, very poor bunt was laid down the third-base line. Instead of focusing on what I wished I had, I was learning to enjoy the game that I'd loved since I was a child, the game that somehow, in the midst of being an "adult," I had managed to forget.

While watching the game with my dad, I would listen as he'd get on his soapbox about all manner of baseball topics, guiding me through subtleties of the game that I had never fully appreciated before. He'd go on about things like the shift. The shift is when a dead-pull slugger such as Ted Williams steps up to the plate, everyone in the ballpark knows where he's hitting it. Have you ever seen Teddy Ballgame hit a grounder to the opposite field? Neither did most teams, and they eventually wised up and moved the second baseman to shallow right field, the shortstop behind and maybe a shade to the right of second base, and the third baseman a shade to the left of second. That way, if Williams didn't pull it in the air, it was probably going to the right side on the ground, right at one of the perfectly positioned infielders. We saw this same defensive strategy with Barry Bonds, and more currently we see it with Jason Giambi, Jim Thome, and Carlos Delgado. It's almost always executed against a left-handed pull hitter with pop. I can't recall it being used against a righty; seems awkward, since you'd need your first baseman covering the bag.

But that's pretty specific defensive strategy right there. Usually, we just see the defense—at least the infield—play straight away. If a runner is on third and it's late in the game, we'll see the infield move in to the lip of the grass, intending to come home with a ground ball. Other times, if there are men on first and third and it's late, we'll see the corners come in and the shortstop and second baseman inch a little closer to second. That way, if the ball is hit to first or third, the fielder can grab it quickly, look the runner back to third, and still have time to turn a double play. The trick is to turn two without the runner on third scoring. Rarely does it work. The run usually scores. But A for effort.

The more I learned about things like the shift, the more I started to check out the small pieces of fabric that make the game flow. How the outfield plays specific hitters or, on an even more subtle note, how the outfield plays a runner on second. First, the hitter. Just like Ted Williams was a dead-pull hitter, there are many players who, more often than not, go the opposite way. Wade Boggs was like this, and so is Derek Jeter. Next time you get a chance, watch how Derek pulls his hands in toward his body on an inside pitch. He's making sure he doesn't get jammed by finding a way, no matter how awkward it looks, to get the bat head on the ball. You don't see him break many bats, and that's because he's so good with his hands. So how do you defend against that? Well, you look at who's pitching, and if he's someone who brings it hard and in,

Jeter's challenge that day will be to fight it off, and if he's successful, he'll be dropping the ball into right field. My advice to the defense would be to expect the ball on the right side.

But if you've got a slow runner on second, such as any of the three Molina brothers, your right fielder can play deeper. The right fielder, such as Ichiro Suzuki, has a strong arm and therefore can play a little deeper to cover an extra-base hit and still get the ball in for the play at the plate. But if you've got Shane Victorino on second, Ryan Church, another right fielder with a strong arm, will have to rush his throw to get the Flyin' Hawaiian at the plate.

Of course, the shortstop can inch closer to second and fake like he's going to try to pick off Victorino. That will keep him honest, make sure he doesn't get a good lead or a great jump. Baseball is a game of inches, so any little movement here or a fake there could make the difference.

I also began to watch the patterns pitchers use to attack hitters. Like, are you trying to pound him in or make him chase away? If Greg Maddux works the inside half of the plate against David Wright, that sets up the outside half for the next time Wright comes up against Maddux. Wright will probably have gone back to the dugout after the at bat thinking about the pitches he just saw. The next time he faces Maddux, Wright will probably say something to himself like, "Okay, he threw me a 2–0 fastball inside for a strike last time, and it's 2–0 again now, so I should look for a fastball on the inside half."

Maddux, because he is the thinking man's pitcher, will probably be reading Wright's mind and throw it on the outer half of the plate, having set it up by going inside during the previous at bat. But if Maddux pushes the count to 2–0, he also has the option of staying inside with a fastball. He got the strike last time, and who's to say it won't happen again? After all, just because Wright knows it's coming doesn't mean he can put it into play.

I like it when everyone in the ballpark knows what pitch is coming, including the hitter, but it's such a nasty pitch that no one could ever touch it. Think of Sandy Koufax. His out pitch was the four-seam fastball. This pitch gives the appearance of rising in the strike zone, but the reality is that it's just thrown with a lot of backspin and doesn't change planes until late. Keep in mind that pitchers are throwing on a downward angle because the mound is raised; the four seamer just looks like it's rising when the backspin is just keeping it up there a little longer. Anyway, when Koufax needed a strikeout, everyone knew what pitch was coming. And more often than not, the batter wouldn't be able to hit it. Strike three. Take a seat. Better luck next time.

It's when you start noticing these subtleties of the game that you realize baseball is actually a series of games within a game. It's like the game grows within itself. The events are all interconnected, and as you become aware of them all, the game pulls you in deeper. And there comes a point in a fan's life when the game becomes all-encompassing. It's nearly impossible to look away, and suddenly the job phone call that you didn't get that day, the date that ended in disaster—all those other things that felt so important an hour ago have disappeared.

My career mattered, I knew, and so did dating. But in the

heat of the moment, none of it mattered as much as the suicide squeeze. None of it could top a close score, late in the game, when the runner on third breaks as soon as the pitcher begins his movement toward the plate. The runner sprints full tilt. The batter is bunting, intending to sacrifice his at bat in order to drive in the run. But he has to make contact. Miss, and the runner is left out to dry. Often, when the runner breaks, the infielders will holler and the pitcher, knowing the batter must make contact, will throw at the batter's head. If the batter ducks, the runner will be caught. But if he stays tough, doesn't flinch, and makes contact, it is one of the most exciting plays in the game.

"Watch, Lyss, this is important!" my dad would shout during games (even if we were listening to Vin Scully on the radio). "Watch where the infielders positioned themselves for the cutoff throw. Watch the first baseman moving in behind the guy at first base, and how the pitcher knows when to try a pickoff move. Watch to see whether the infielders are playing for a double play.

"Watch! This is important!"

And it was important. Not because I was trying to make my dad happy or because I needed the company. It was important because I learned to be happy where I was. It was important because I became a different kind of fan. I became more than simply a tourist passing through a season; I was an active participant in every game.

The more I watched, of course, the more I learned, and it started to change my perspective not just on the individual games, but also on the sport as a whole. Baseball is the only sport where the team with possession of the ball is actually on defense. Think about it. In soccer, football, ice hockey, if you have the ball (or puck), you're on offense. Not so in baseball. To get on base and ultimately to score is an exercise in reaction. An obvious truth, perhaps, but somewhat buried beneath the surface.

It's the only sport where the complex web of communication that lurks beneath the surface does not require microphones, where play calling is done through gesture alone. Sign language. Signals. The third-base coach touches the brim of his hat, his nose, his ear, his hat, ear, nose, ear, then drags his hand across his belt. What the hell was that? Well, depending on the team's signals, that could have been a sign for a delayed steal, a bunt, or, commonly, nothing at all.

And yet despite these signals' quick pace and brevity, some teams are able to steal their opponent's signs. It baffled me that summer, and still does today. There is so much tacit communication going on during a game, how could anyone make heads or tails of another team's signs? That just speaks to the patterns found in a game. If the third-base coach touches his elbow and nose during one at bat and the base runner steals second, then later the third-base coach touches his elbow and hat and the base runner steals again, chances are that the elbow is the directive to steal. Most of the time, the information that is communicated with slight hand gestures during a game is far more complicated than what I'm talking about. This is what my brother learned in Little League. But when teams change their signs in the middle of a game, sometimes they have to keep them simple.

For example, when Pedro Martinez looks in to Brian Schneider for the sign and Schneider flashes the index finger, convention says a fastball is coming. Batters know better than to sneak a peek at the catcher when he's signaling the pitcher. They may just find the next pitch in their ear. That doesn't prevent runners on second base from trying to peer in and see what digits are popping up in the catcher's crotch. With a runner on second, the batter usually uses a different set of signs, including an indicator and a nullifier. If one was a fastball, with a runner on second, the catcher might flash one three times to indicate fastball, the first two being indicators; but if he follows it up with two twos, the pitch is off, nullified by the prearranged double twos; the next sign is three, which is a slider, so let's just go with that now. Confused? So's the runner on second.

What I learned is that baseball isn't what happens after the pitch is thrown and the ball is hit. It's about the moments in between. The quiet *before* the pitcher throws a pitch. When the ball is in the air. That's when the magic happens. That's where strategy is revealed. That's what lends itself to the drama. My brother, Cory, is the person who clued me into that.

Home runs are great, and exciting, and I cry whenever a Dodger hits one to win a game in the bottom of the ninth or in extra innings. I like home runs. But I love small ball. I've told people that before, said, "This chick loves the small ball." (That's gotten me in trouble when the other person isn't a baseball fan, but that's another story.) Small ball is the game of strategy, the thinking behind the double steal, and the suicide squeeze, and why one player is going to lay down a drag bunt and another will always swing away. This chick loves small ball and all the obsessive thinking and predictions that go along with it. I love trying to figure out what's going to happen next, and why what did happen happened.

I love trying to understand the total weirdness of Nomar Garciaparra, not only because of his pre–at bat OCD but because without fail, no matter what, he always swings at the first pitch he sees, which is always, without fail, no matter what, a fastball down the middle. I never could figure that out. Nor could I figure out why he would then swing at the next couple pitches that came his way, always curveballs way out of the strike zone.

Predicting what's going to happen in a baseball game is almost as much fun as watching what's happening. Does your team call for a bunt with a man on and nobody out, even though the hitter is hitting .420 the past month? Do you challenge the best hitter in the league with a fastball and a base open, because he's in a slump, or walk him to get to the number five hitter, even though that guy's been hitting everything lately? Do you try to move a runner over, or swing away? Do you bring in a reliever, or let your starter try to get out of trouble?

If you know your players and your manager well enough, you can usually have a pretty good idea of how a play's going to unfold. After that summer I started to read the field, follow the count, and make predictions of my own. At first I was wrong a lot, but since then, I've started being right a hell of a lot more.

I've been watching regularly for the past six years and

learning. I've learned that the game has changed a lot since it was first played in 1871. I've learned how the pitchers mound was lowered, and how, as the world became more specialized, so did baseball—that pitchers going nine innings is about as common in the contemporary era as wool uniforms. Some of the changes seemed good (who can't appreciate the sheer inventiveness demonstrated by shortstops bouncing throws to first base when they're in a hurry) and some not so good (like instant replay and Astroturf).

But what seems constant to me amid all the change is how the appeal of the game remains the same. That's partly because even with all the changes, it's still a game of balls and strikes, of hits and outs, of wins and losses. But the constant appeal is also because of how baseball touches us in different ways, at different times in our lives. When we're very young, it might be about spectacle and bright lights and candy, a few hours on Dad's lap, or sitting next to Mom. As we get older, it's about heroes and villains, victories and defeat, a simple oasis in our difficult lives. And then we reach a point—or at least I did—when enjoying the game gets more complicated because life gets more complicated. However, instead of compromising the purity of the game, those complications deepen its appeal and heighten the sense of what it means to be a fan.

When the game finds you at the right time, you don't really have a choice; you just have to heed the call. If you're paying attention, answering that call can mean the difference between pulling yourself out of a rut and letting it go on indefinitely. The pull of the game really is that strong if you're willing to commit. The fact that FDR encouraged baseball to continue even during the Great Depression should tell you something. It's our national antidepressant for a reason.

Without even knowing it, I reached a point that a lot of fans do, a point where we all meet—all the statistics keepers and talk-show fans and television screamers and the fantasy-league managers. We watch an old game, an old game with new changes every year, and we forget our own lives, and then we find that our lives have somehow been incorporated into the game. It's not just us trying to discern whether the way a pitcher shrugs his left shoulder means he's about to make a pickoff move, or whether it just means he's got an itch. It's a lot of people. A lot of fans. Some of that I learned on my own. But a lot I learned from others.

Learning the game from someone creates—or cements—a bond that will last your entire life. Teaching it to someone else does the same thing, because you never know what's going on in someone's life or how she might need baseball without even knowing it. My assistant, who is also my friend, is named Kelly. She's figuring out her professional and personal future, worrying about money and boyfriends and life. And when I go on and on about this pitcher's off-speed stuff or that batter's tendency to pull the ball, she rolls her eyes.

When I watch a game with her, I do for her just what others have done for me.

"Now watch this next pitch," I say. "Because the batter's going to bunt." And he does.

Kelly looks at me somewhat shocked and says, "How did you *know* that?"

"I'll teach you," I tell her. And I will.

chapter seven

The Art and Science of Being a Fan

*I only had one superstition. I made sure to touch
all the bases when I hit a home run.*

—BABE RUTH

When I go to a game, my routine looks something like this: I pick out something to wear, discover it's in the dirty-clothes hamper, and pick out something else. I tend to be pretty selective about what I wear to the ballpark. Would you wear a pair of ratty jeans and a college sweatshirt to church or to the opera? (That's assuming you're the kind of person who would go to the opera in the first place.) You're going to the ballpark to relax, sure, but you're also going to worship at the altar of excellence, to join a community that is cheering for the same higher power (the Dodgers, in my case) that you cheer for. So I try to look nice.

After I've picked out what to wear, I grab my Dodgers cap and get in the car with my dad and my brother and, every once in a while, my mother, who claims she's not a big fan and still to this day can't read the scoreboard. When we're in the car, we have our first argument. Should we take Olympic or Third? Should we try that exit or this one? How do we beat the traffic? (This is L.A., after all.) Just because we go to at least forty games a year doesn't mean that we can agree on the best way to get there. This driving debate is the first in a series of heated conversations that usually unfold in the following order:

1. Is Joe Torre going to start Andruw Jones?

   Answer: Hmm, tough call. Has he been 1-for-23 with runners in scoring position over the last six games? He has? Okay, then there's probably a fifty–fifty chance.

2. Is Jeff Kent going to run like he's got a piano on his back?

   Answer: Yes, Jeff Kent will always run like he's got a piano on his back—especially if it matters.

3. Will Hiroki Kuroda make it through the fourth inning?

Answer: Let's hope so; otherwise, my voice will probably give out sometime around the sixth inning.

And the whole time, we're listening to my brother's playlist, the one he made just for Dodgers games. My brother's a music editor, and he makes playlists for everything—for parties, for birthdays, for hot dates, for funerals. Basically, he scores our lives. It's honestly the best mix that you're ever going to hear on your way to a Dodgers game. It's got a Vin Scully announcement of a Sandy Koufax no-hitter, along with the following:

"I Love Mickey"—*Teresa Brewer and Mickey Mantle*

"Right Field"—*Peter, Paul, and Mary*

"Did You See Jackie Robinson Hit That Ball?"—*Count Basie*

"Say Hey The Willie Mays Song"—*The Treniers*

"Dodger Blue"—*Dave Frishberg*

"Mrs. Robinson"—*Simon and Garfunkel*

"Cory Snyder"—*The Farmhands*

"Joltin' Joe DiMaggio"—*Les Brown and His Orchestra*

"Baseball Boogie"—*Mabel Scott*

"Catfish"—*Bob Dylan*

"Willie, Mickey & the Duke (Talkin' Baseball)"—*Terry Cashman*

"Piazza, New York Catcher"—*Belle and Sebastian*

"Knock the Cover off the Ball"—*Randy Newman*

Okay, so the playlist is maybe a little over the top, but it's still a lovable practice. I know families who sing "Take Me Out to the Ballgame" every time they go to a game. I have a group of girlfriends who wouldn't think of driving to a game without their lucky socks. A little odd? Trust me, these are nice socks (and they work). The point is, it's a ritual. It's special. It's a family tradition; thus, you are supposed to feel slightly ridiculous while engaging in it.

Usually by the time we're on "Baseball Boogie," we're close to the stadium. No matter how many outfits I had to sort through, how bad traffic was, or how fierce our arguing about the size of the piano on Jeff Kent's back, we've always left enough time to make it there half an hour before the first pitch. We park in our usual spot, and we walk right behind home plate, to the Dugout Club. That's when I have my moment with Jackie Robinson. And afterward, we take our seats.

Getting there early is important because, as with all things baseball, it's the instances that surround the action that lend the event its power and its appeal. The anticipation and ritual before the game are almost as crucial as the game itself. I find this is true for anything that's important, whether it's cooking a hamburger or buying a new pair of shoes or going on a date. Anticipation, preparation, fantasizing . . . and celebration or disappointment, depending. All of these are important for a game where the action itself is such a small (but critical) part of the entire tapestry of strategy and preparation.

Just as there's no better time to watch a player than when he's in the on-deck circle, to study his facial expression and his body language, to examine his every twitch and shrug, there's no better opportunity to check the vibes on your team than before a game. Not that either will necessarily give away anything valuable, or that you'll actually be able to ascertain anything terribly wise about what's going to happen. But keen, loving attention is what being a fan is all about. It's the *study* of the game, and the players. The real horse racing fan loves hanging out at the track, likes nothing better than to study the jockeys and trainers and groomsmen, looking for subtle hints as to how the big brown stud in the third race is feeling. The bird-watcher comes alive when a red-breasted nuthatch comes into view. But that same bird-watcher would still be bird-watching—would be loving his binoculars and his bird-watching books and his bird-watching boots—even if the nuthatch never showed up. A real baseball fan should be just as loyal, should enjoy the pregame vibe just for the *vibiness*. That's why I get there early.

I tell you all this not just because I'm looking for an excuse to make up a word like "vibiness." I realized not long ago that my pregame routine—which I had never given much thought to—carries an obsessiveness and preoccupation with repetition that I think any serious fan will recognize. Some might call it OCD; I call it the art and science of being a fan.

There's something beautiful about the relationship a fan has with his or her team. Something beautiful and intense and, if that person spends all his or her time locked in a basement, watching games on a computer screen or television, or listening on a radio, and never actually visits the ballpark, something a little creepy. Maybe that's a little much. Every serious fan has a close personal relationship with her team and with the game, but if it never becomes anything larger than a personal relationship, then that fan is missing out on something. Going to a game in person gives you the opportunity to feel the slings and arrows of outrageous baseball fortune along with a group of like-minded people. That's why sports bars are always packed. That's why you always hear how a day at the ballpark is a great family activity. And that's why I have season tickets.

Obviously, I have some strong feelings about fandom. Partly, that's because I have strong feelings about just about everything. I guess it shouldn't surprise anyone that I bring this zealousness to my fan-ness as well. Being a fan to me is not just about how you act and watch when you're at the stadium, it's about what you do at home. How you react when bad news steps into the batter's box, and how you celebrate when you get two on, no out in the top of the seventh. This isn't about superstition, though that's part of it. This is about something else. This is about the habitual things you do that make any game that much better.

If you're already a fan, you know what works for you, and you probably know what fan mistakes to avoid. If you're not a fan yet, and want to be, here are a few things I've learned to use in my living room or the bleacher seats:

Take It Personally

If you're a fan, you care. If you care, you hurt when your team loses. I just hope you don't hurt as much as my dad does. My mom, dad, and I were at my house during an away game last season, listening to the game on the radio, and it was the seventh inning, and we were losing 5–2. Suddenly my dad got up and said, "I can't do this anymore, I just can't take it. I'm a Cubs fan now. The Dodgers are dead to me."

Well, my mom and I had heard stuff like this before—my dad's an emotional guy—so we weren't too worried. And we weren't too worried when, after the Dodgers lost 5–3, my dad slammed a few doors and grumbled something about heartbreak and how he was too old for this.

"He gets so upset when we lose," my mom said to me. "I don't know what to do with him." And I was thinking, "Duh!" but, like I said, wasn't too worried, because I was focusing on my own lousy mood, and hoping the top of the order would start hitting soon.

I started worrying the next day when I heard my dad calling his dog. You see, his dog's name is Dodger, except he didn't call it Dodger. Instead he yelled, "Here, Cubbie. C'mere, Cubbie, you're my little winner."

Now you're probably thinking to yourself, "Aw, that's cute and funny," but the thing to keep in mind is that he was serious. I'm pretty sure that if the Dodgers had continued down that path for too long, we would have had to retrain Dodger to respond to a different name, so long as that name was not in the National League. (Luckily for us and for the dog, our team started hitting again. Dodger the dog is Dodger the dog once more.)

I take it personally too, but instead of changing my dog's name from Gibson to Pujols, I just weep. Actually, between you and me, my brother weeps too. After the Dodgers were eliminated by the Phillies in the playoffs in 2008, my brother and I cried like babies. It got so bad that a couple of strangers came over to hug and console us. True story.

If You're Going to Be Cruel, Be Cool

My brother is probably the greatest heckler in the world because he understands that the great hecklers aren't trying to unsettle players. The great hecklers know that the players are pros, and that if they could be thrown by some loudmouth with a baseball ticket, they probably never would have made it to the big leagues.

This is why a few years ago when Ricky Ledee struck out looking during a crucial at bat with a playoff spot on the line, my brother, who's usually not so loud, said pretty loudly, "Why'd you even bring the bat?" as Ledee was heading into the dugout. As Ricky Ledee disappeared into the dugout we saw him smile and shake his head.

Another time we scored some really good seats at Shea Stadium, and David Wright, who had heard I was there, was very intent on finding me in the stands. Watching him crane his neck around, my brother yelled loud enough for Wright to hear: "Focus, David, the game is over there."

During the All-Star Game in 2007 A-Rod was wearing pure white wristbands and pure white sneakers. Seats on the third-base line. A-Rod at third. "Wh-ite snea-kers" caught on in the entire section thanks to my brother.

Perhaps his best heckling, though, happens on our home turf at Dodger Stadium. Andruw Jones is what old sportswriters would call "stout," what Vin Scully calls "a big boy," and what unimaginative hecklers call "Tubby" or "Lardass."

Not my brother.

"Come on, Snacks!" my brother yelled. "You can do it, Snacks!"

I doubt whether Sna . . . I mean, Jones, heard my brother, but that wasn't the point.

What I've learned from my brother and others like him is that the real heckler artists aren't playing to the players, they're playing to the fans around them. Good heckling is more for the people around you, for entertainment value, than it is for the people on the teams. My brother's not a screamer, which makes him a great heckler. He's not trying to embarrass you, just trying to amuse the people around us.

My father's another story. He loves to embarrass me. If someone from the Dodgers gets picked off at second, he'll yell, really loud, "Well, that didn't work too well, did it?"

Not that embarrassing, you say? Well, you haven't heard my father yelling. Yelling in ballparks is all about the delivery.

You can be next to someone who says the worst things, but if he or she says them at a volume that only you and the guy in front of you can hear, it's not really that bad. Then again, you can be next to someone like my father who will broadcast whatever he's thinking as loudly as possible at any given moment, causing you to hide your face in embarrassment.

Even though it embarrasses me, I let him yell loudly for three reasons:

1. Because he likes to and it wouldn't be the same game without it.

2. At least when he yells, the words that come out of his mouth are pretty creative. You will never catch my father uttering a bland taunt.

3. Creative taunts are contagious. A lot of times one good heckler will bring out the best in everyone. Even if it makes one person say something more interesting than "You suck!" or "You're a moron!" it's worth it.

I guess we just never totally grow out of that teenager-who's-embarrassed-by-her-parents phase. To put it another way, I've spoken to players on the Dodgers who've made me blush when they've said slightly backhanded things to me like, "I see you sitting with your dad. He seems really . . . uh . . . passionate."

Passionate. Yeah, that's exactly what he is. Apple trees make apples.

Wild Pitch When These Fans Said They Would Kill for Their Team, They Weren't Kidding

Cubs fans live and die with their team. And in June 1949, one fan took that passion beyond reasonable levels. Eddie Waitkus joined the Cubs in 1941 before leaving for military duty shortly thereafter. He returned to the ballfield in 1946, promptly taking over the starting job at first base.

In 1948, he had an All-Star season. But the Cubs needed pitching, and after the season, they traded the popular Waitkus to the Phillies for two starting pitchers, Dutch Leonard and Monk Dubiel. Most of the North Side of Chicago wallowed in misery with Waitkus's departure, but none more so than Ruth Ann Steinhagen. She was an impressionable eleven-year-old girl in 1941, when Waitkus made his debut.

When Waitkus returned to Chicago on June 14, 1949, as a member of the Phillies, he was hitting .306 and was sure to repeat as an All-Star selection. But after the game, a vindicating 9–2 Phillies victory, he received a note from Ruth Ann, now a nineteen-year-old hottie, encouraging him to come to her room.

Now, for what it's worth, there are reports that Waitkus's girlfriend was also named Ruth Ann, and who knows, maybe he thought she was in town for a surprise. But when he knocked on the door and not-his-girlfriend invited him in, he accepted.

The details of the following moments vary, as you can probably imagine, but the meat of the story is that Ruth Ann directed Waitkus to stand by the window and said, "For two years you've been bothering me, and now you're going to die." Then she shot him in the chest with a rifle. As he lay there dying and drowning and gurgling in his own blood, she phoned the front desk and confessed to what had happened. Paramedics came, and while the bullet missed his heart and all his major organs, he surely would have died had he not received immediate medical treatment. Her phone call probably saved his life.

She was charged with attempted murder but served only three years in a mental institution. Waitkus returned to baseball but was never the same.

You may recognize this story. Bernard Malamud fictionalized Waitkus's experience into a major scene—and theme—in his 1952 novel *The Natural*. It was made into a movie in 1984, starring Robert Redford, and is my pick for best all-time baseball movie, next to *Bull Durham*.

Waitkus wasn't the only ballplayer who felt the wrath of a woman scorned. In 1932, Billy Jurges was a solid shortstop (also with the Cubs) with a weakish bat in his second big-league season. (His

Not quite my black leotard and pink tights but close. While growing up on Staten Island, I would often dance and entertain my family, with the ever-present sound of a Yankees game on TV in the background.

After my first professional acting job as part of the cast of *Annie*, my brother was born. It didn't take long for us to start watching games together, and we've been doing it ever since.

When I was cast in *Who's the Boss*, my parents made the difficult decision that my father and I would move out west so that I could tape the first season, leaving my mother and brother behind in New York City for the time being. My dad played first base for the *Who's the Boss* softball team, which featured Tony Danza as the pitcher.

Along with my father, my brother was a huge reason why I fell in love with this game. As a result, baseball has long been the ultimate in Milano family entertainment.

My father and brother today. One look at this picture and you can see that they clearly get a lot of pleasure out of embarrassing me at the park.

One key to being a great fan: Never underestimate your mother. She may not be the most vocal fan in my family, but she definitely knows her stuff.

The pastime's past time—never forget the legends and the stories that have made this game what it is. Ernie Banks (LEFT) and Ozzie Smith (RIGHT) are two of the greatest to ever play.

Willie Mays. There's nothing else to say except "Wow."

Here I am talking to Tony La Russa. Talking to managers is an amazing way to learn more about the game, but if you ever get the chance, just remember that they don't always want to hear what you *really* think about the job they're doing.

All I want for Christmas is a win in the World Series! The Dodgers' original Santa Claus, Tommy Lasorda.

Though I am a Dodgers fan, I can always appreciate baseball talent wherever I see it. Derek Jeter is one of the best shortstops to ever play the game.

I'm a sucker for mascots.

Nomar has been one of my favorite players ever since he arrived from Chicago. Along with his OCD batting routine, he has become a fixture in the Dodgers' lineup.

In this picture I'm with the Cardinals closer in 2008, Ryan Franklin.

Just being in the same ballpark with Hank Aaron gave me the chills.

The 2007 All-Star game. Brad Penny from the Dodgers was pitching.

Being a goodwill ambassador for UNICEF changed my life in the best way possible. As if that wasn't enough, it also gave me a new perspective on baseball and what it meant to me.

My Chihuahua, Gibson. His name speaks for itself.

My parents' dog, Dodger. Despite the fact that my dad began calling him "Cubbie" during a poor hitting display by the Dodgers, he thankfully still answers to the name Dodger.

Russell Martin, the Dodgers catcher. He's a player I've been watching ever since his rookie year, and he's returned my loyalty by calling a lot of great games. He better not leave.

Joe Mauer, the catcher from the Twins. What can I say, catchers are a good group to hang around with.

If I could drop it all, forget acting, and do whatever I wanted, I'd probably travel to every ballpark with my brother. As it is, we've been to a bunch: (FROM TOP TO BOTTOM) Petco Park in San Diego, Fenway in Boston, Shea in New York, and PNC Park in Pittsburgh are just a few.

A picture of when Brad Penny invited me to the batting cage under Dodger Stadium after a game. He pretty much had me at "Let's go down to the clubhouse."

The fact that I just got to swing the bat in the same place where Kirk Gibson warmed up before he hit his legendary home run was enough for me. With a little help from Eric Gagne, I was able to hit Brad's pitch and avoid the strikeout.

Before the 2007 season, I partnered with MLB to launch my MLB-branded clothing line, Touch. Suddenly I had a new outlet and way to share my love of the game with all the other fans out there who make baseball the best sport there is.

Through Touch, I began traveling to ballparks and hosting merchandise-signing events across the country. Everywhere I went I was so impressed by the die-hard female fans I met who were eager to support their team by wearing colors that weren't pink.

In the fall of 2007, because of my blogging and connection to Touch, I did some playoff coverage for TBS, which gave me the chance to get behind the scenes of some terrific ballparks. This picture was taken under the stands at Chase Field, home of the Diamondbacks, where I did a story on their kids' area.

I interviewed Colorado Rockies player Jeff Francis for TBS during their exciting and unexpected run to the 2007 World Series.

Here I am with the members of the Colorado Rockies' ground crew. Coors Field is an impeccable ballpark, and the crew does an amazing job to keep it that way.

Chase Field has a VIP pool in the outfield. I can honestly say that it's the only park I've seen with this feature.

I've been lucky enough to talk to all kinds of sports personalities in my pursuit to share my love of the game with anyone and everyone. This is me doing a Boston-area radio show.

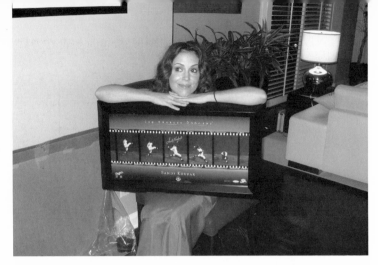

My 2007 birthday present and perhaps my most prized piece of memorabilia: a photo series of Sandy Koufax that was signed by the man himself.

My father. You can take the man and the Dodgers out of Brooklyn, but you can never take the Brooklyn Dodgers out of the man.

This is my dad on his way into a game at the Los Angeles Coliseum to mark the fiftieth anniversary of the Dodgers moving to Los Angeles. The irony was not wasted on either of us. If I'd told him thirty years ago that he'd be at a game devoted to the celebration of the Dodgers moving out of Brooklyn, he never would have believed me. But hey, that's the power of baseball.

Manny fever officially infiltrated the Milano cheering section during the second half of the 2008 season.

The 2008 playoffs. Though it didn't work out this year, I'm still waiting for a new tale of playoff greatness to become a part of Dodger lore.

The entire Milano clan at the 2008 All-Star game at Yankee Stadium. One of the rare occasions that we were all together. It's not all that surprising that baseball made it happen.

lifetime batting average was .258 in seventeen seasons.) On July 6, Violet Valli (née Popovich), a showgirl and former girlfriend of Jurges's, visited him at the Carlos Hotel in Chitown, where Cubbies stayed during home games, with a gun. Whether he wrestled it from her before or after she fired is unclear, but fire she did. She had brought a suicide note, too, indicating her twisted dream of murder-suicide. But Jurges survived (and went on to a long career as an All-Star shortstop, then a manager). Not only that, but he refused to press charges against the showgirl. Violet? She signed a twenty-two-week contract to sing at local nightclubs and theaters, and was billed as "Violet, What I Did for Love, Valli, the Most Talked About Girl in Chicago." After that, who knows?

Whenever I hear a family member or friend say, after watching a great catch or a perfect double steal or a bizarre hop, "That's unbelievable!" I think of Billy and Vi. *That* was unbelievable.

★

Bring the Right Tools

I always plan to bring a transistor radio, and always forget. The transistor is perfect for all those moments when you don't know exactly what happened, or what's happening— like when there's a rhubarb between a third-base coach and

the home plate ump. When that happens, I'm always thinking, "I wish I could be listening to Vin tell me what's going
on." I express my frustration by yelling, "What's your beef,
Snacks?" That almost always fits at least one of the people
arguing.

You want a glove in case there's a pop-up, certainly, and, a
lot of times in the early part of the season, a blanket. Binoculars, sure. Other than that, I don't think there should be any
more props. Baseball's more than a hundred years old, and it
got along fine without those things before. I don't think
people should read during games either. Although once my
mom, during the rare game she came along with my brother
and dad and me, brought a newspaper. When I saw what she
was reading, I couldn't get too mad. It was the sports section.

Know Where Your Team Is From

Baseball has been an international game for a long time now,
and currently there are a lot of players who weren't born here
who chose to call this game and our country home. Part of
what makes this game great is that this multiculturalism
exposes you to people from countries that you might not otherwise have known. When a foreign-born player joins your
team, suddenly you've got not only a new player to learn
about, but a new country as well.

This diversity has been going on for a while, but it's really
kicked into high gear in the last twenty to thirty years. The
sport became more globally directed in 1980 when Fernando
Valenzuela, a nineteen-year-old Mexican left-hander, took

the mound for the Dodgers. The Latin population in California was surging, and "El Toro" became an icon in the Los Angeles Hispanic community. Valenzuela lived up to the challenge. In 1981, his proper rookie season, he went 13–7 in 25 starts with a 2.48 ERA, after starting the season 8–0 with a 0.50 ERA, and he finished with 180 strikeouts in 192⅓ innings pitched. He won the Rookie of the Year and Cy Young awards and finished fifth in the MVP voting. In 1990, one of his last great seasons, Valenzuela threw a no-hitter against the St. Louis Cardinals. His number 34 is not retired by the Dodgers but is not among available numbers, either.

Use this diversity to help cheer for your team. Perhaps the next Dominican hotshot player will win the Triple Crown with your fans' support.

Plug into Your Team

Clearly, in these modern times, there are a lot of ways to stay tuned into what's going on with your team. Some people are partial to *SportsCenter,* others prefer to keep up online, and still others prefer *SportsCenter* online. Whether your method is the local news, the sports page, or sports talk radio, follow your team. Know the batting order and the pitching rotation. Is there some hot prospect that just got bumped up from AAA? Is your second baseman 3-for-30 in the last six games? These are things that you need to know in order to call yourself a fan.

Personally my routine goes something like this: I try to watch as many games as I can, usually at least a couple a week. Sometimes my schedule doesn't let me do that, so I also try to catch *SportsCenter* or watch highlights online if that happens. On the Internet, I check out DodgerDugout. com and the blogs on MLBlogs.com. I read the message boards on the official Dodgers Web site to see what other fans are saying. I read the sports section of the *L.A. Times*. I like reading T. J. Simers's column, although he never seems to have anything nice to say. (I keep reading it with hopes that someday he might.) I listen to MLB Home Plate on XM satellite radio. I check out rumors and hot stove reports.

Recently I signed up for the Dodgers text alerts on my phone, which have become a good way for me to keep up, but they can also drive me crazy. Like when I'm watching the game on TV, an opposing batter hits a home run to take the lead, and then my cell phone beeps with a text message saying that the Dodgers blew it. It's like my cell phone is taunting me. I never knew a cell phone could pour salt in the wound until I signed up for this service.

Know When to Stand

Some parks around the country have this great rule: If there's a play going on, you're not allowed to go to your seat. I love that. I'm a big, big, big supporter of waiting until someone's out of his batting stance before you go to your seat. You should wait till the action is done. That goes for any kind of hot dog or pop-corn ordering from the ballpark people too. When someone's getting a beer in front of me, and something's happening on the field, I'll yell at him to get a seat.

And then there are times when I don't care what anyone is yelling—I'm standing. You know, when you have two outs and your closer's out there. You've got to stand up for that last out. How could you not? And we always participate in the seventh-inning stretch. We sway back and forth with our arms around each other. Even if your team loses, you can't be unhappy to be at the ballpark for a night.

The Eating Ritual

Going to a baseball game is a total sensory experience. The sights. The sounds. The smells. The tastes. Every sense has something specific to explore and enjoy. I also find that each ballpark has its own specific look, sound, smell, and food. Dodger Stadium is unique to me. You know how your home is unique in that sensory way? It has that smell that exemplifies home. Well, I feel your home ballpark is unique too. No two ballparks smell the same, and there's no place like home.

I usually start off at the buffet table in the Dugout Club. Sometimes I order a veggie burger. Other times I get just salad. By the fourth inning, I eat nachos, with just cheese and guacamole, and then in the sixth I usually eat something sweet. If it is a cold night I will get some hot chocolate. And much like when you eat at the same restaurant often and you get the same thing every time you're there, I stick to the same basic items at every game regardless of what's available. I think it may be a superstition at this point. "What if I get the veggie wrap instead of the veggie burger and they lose? I better stick to the veggie burger." I'm kidding. Sort of.

Language!

You want to be fanatical, but keep things in perspective. This is a family sport, and there are kids around. Pay attention to the words that come out of your mouth. I definitely think there should be no cursing. If you're going to curse, and sometimes the game actually inspires that behavior, do it under your breath and into your beer cup. If someone's drinking too much, report it to security if it's getting really obnoxious.

Does that mean I don't curse? Hell no! I'll curse out a player. I'll curse him out in language you wouldn't believe. But I'll do it in my head. What's even crazier, sometimes I'll do it to a favorite player, before he steps up to the plate, to telepathically motivate him into proving me wrong. Fan logic is twisted, no?

When in Rome . . .

If you're going to invite someone who is a fan of the opposing team, he needs rules, because he's in your house now. It's a matter of consideration. I understand flying the colors for your team. But I don't understand why anyone would wear a Cubs hat to a Cardinals game in St. Louis. That's nuts. We went to Fenway last year for a Yankees–Red Sox game, but my brother, instead of wearing a Yankees jersey, wore a Dodgers Garciaparra shirt, and the Red Sox fans respected that. I think there are ways to be creative in someone else's ballpark, ways that show respect but that still maintain your dignity.

Love Your (Play-by-Play) Man

If you're a real fan, one of the most important people in your life is the radio play-by-play man; someday, maybe it will be a woman. He's the guy who (on those nights you're not at the ballpark) lets you see the hanging curve, and watch as it's whacked over the center-field wall. He's the guy who lets you watch the pitcher shake the home run off, and dust the next batter with a high fastball. He's the guy who makes you witness the shortstop dive deep into the hole and makes an impossible stop of a sizzling ground ball while falling to his knees, then whirl and, still on the ground, makes an *impossible* throw, and the runner is . . . *out!*

If he's good, he makes you see all that. If he's great, he makes you feel it. Chicago fans I know tell me that Harry Caray was great, and friends from St. Louis swear that no one will ever approach the magisterial effortlessness of Jack Buck. Philadelphia has Harry Kalas, and in Atlanta, mention Skip Caray, son of Harry, and it's like you're talking about a best friend. But for me, there's only one announcer.

I could tell you about his wit and his descriptive powers and his unabashed and never-forced love of the game. But if you don't know those things already, you've never listened to Vin Scully. And if you have, then you already know.

My mother calls him Vincent. As in, "I was listening to Vincent last night," or "Vincent says that Torre seems to be good for the clubhouse." The other day, my brother was telling me that the Dodgers were about to call up a hot hitting prospect from their farm team.

"How'd you know that?" I asked him.

"Vin told me."

When your family members are referring to your play-by-play man by his full name, or mentioning him the same way you might mention an uncle or close friend, then you have exactly the right relationship with him. If, on the other hand, comments about him range from "I can't stand that blowhard" to "I'd rather watch the game with the volume turned down" to "Who *cares* what you think?" (yelled in the direction of the radio), then you're in trouble. Turn down the volume. Buy the games on the Internet.

Make Some Rules for Watching the Game

In my house, no one can stand when the ball's in play. And in the bottom of the ninth, when the home team is up, no talking *or* eating. Controlling, you say? Type A? No, just a fan. Besides, without rules, where would we be? Robert Frost once said that writing free verse (which is like life without rules, if you ask me) is "like playing tennis with the net down." Sorry, baseball makes me go all poetic. It made even Robert Frost go all poetic. "Poets are like baseball pitchers," the great man said. "Both have their moments. The intervals are the tricky things."

Don't Make Too Many Rules

In the end, baseball is about fun, and it's no secret that if you make too many rules, it gets in the way of just about everything. A baseball game, more than any other sport, provides all kinds of opportunities to reflect, to kibitz, to just gab. So let 'em gab. Just make sure they don't decide to debate the relative merits of Coke and Pepsi during the bottom of the ninth with two on and one out.

Never Underestimate Your Mother

My mom couldn't care less about baseball, but she's a mom, and she loves her family, so she'll pretend. That's the way it's always been. At least that's what I always thought. She'll cook a feast if we're having people over to watch a game. Eggplant Parmesan, meatballs, vegetarian pasta (that's for me), rolled lasagna, stuffed artichokes. And she'll nod her head and say mmm-hmm when my dad is going on about how the Dodgers need to improve their starting rotation, or shake her head and smile when my dad asks if the baseball gods are going to curse the Dodgers for his lifetime for leaving Brooklyn.

So when Mom comes along to the ballpark, it's a rare event. Once when she came last year, she was looking through the paper and pretending to look interested, and it was sweet. Late in the game, we were winning, and Joe Beimel, our top lefty reliever, was on the mound. Top of the ninth, one-run lead and one out, and out of nowhere, Mom said, "I love Joe Beimel."

"What?" I said. It's as if a popcorn vendor had started reciting poetry, in Uzbek. I didn't think she even knew who Joe Beimel was. "What'd you say, Mom?"

She said it again. "I love Joe Beimel."

Then I caught on. She was trying to make her family happy.

"Really?" I asked. "Tell me what you love so much about him."

"Didn't he get in trouble last year because he cut open his hand in a bar, then lied and said it happened in his hotel room, then finally came clean and said, 'I wasn't there drinking sodas all night'? And doesn't he have a tattoo on his right shoulder with a New York City skyline and a broken heart?"

My jaw was hanging so low that ten foul balls could have flown into my mouth.

My mom smiled sweetly. "Do you think you're the only woman in this family who's a fan?" she said.

Touché.

chapter eight

Cheating Through the Ages

With lies you may get ahead in the world—
but you can never go back.

—RUSSIAN PROVERB

I think it's safe to say that, going all the way back to kindergarten, no one likes cheaters, especially when it comes to baseball. Baseball is supposed to be about effort and excellence, rule and rigor. I sincerely believe that cheating subverts all of that and makes the game about the person. It's not enough to say that cheating spoils the game or ruins it for everyone.

Here's something else I believe: Cheaters and cheating

have been part of baseball since the first pitcher discovered that a little dab of saliva could make a ball flutter, since the first batter discovered the clout contained in just a little bit of cork.

It's not the cheating that's new, it's the sense these days that it's worse than ever. But it's not worse than ever. It's just . . . different. I think that's because the type of cheating has changed, and because today, cheaters aren't using spit-balls or corked bats, stolen signs or secret pacts. They're using drugs. It used to be, cheaters who got caught got *caught*. Then we could feel righteous anger, and seize the moral high ground and do all the things that society has been doing since it started finding people who didn't play by the rules about, oh, a million years ago. We could brand the cheater with a scarlet letter and basically set out to ruin his life. But now, even when cheaters are caught, the tests aren't always reliable. And even when the tests are reliable, well, maybe they took something without knowing what it was.

People make a huge deal about steroids, and some sports-writers (who, as the steroid mess was unfolding, were either willfully ignorant or allowed themselves to be deceived) get amazingly self-righteous about the players who robbed the game of its innocence. Innocence? I'll talk about the Black Sox in a minute. But first, the fact is that players have always looked for an edge, and I can't say that I blame them. The ambition and responsibility to excel day in and day out are overwhelming. Should it be a surprise that players would look for something to speed healing time, prolong their careers, and make them stronger? The stakes of baseball have always been high, and given the amount of money in the game now, they're higher than ever before.

These days, that missing edge is often to be found in a pill or a needle. We're a pharmaceutical nation, so why should we be surprised when this tendency to solve everything with a magic drug spills over into our sports? In between acts of our favorite shows or on the nightly news, every other commercial is selling a treatment for what ails us. (And might I just add that sporting events are the worst when it comes to this? Next time you watch football on Sunday, count the number of commercials for erectile dysfunction. I can only imagine an eight-year-old asking, "Dad, what's Cialis?") Allergies. Restless leg syndrome (I'm sorry, what?). Cholesterol. Impotence. Pop a pill and we will feel better.

As if this weren't enough, we are also youth obsessed. Creams to make you look younger. Plastic surgery. Botox. In my business, you can't find a woman over forty who hasn't injected herself with something. Those women are looking for the quick fix, looking for ways to extend their careers and maintain their lucrative youth. I can't blame them or fault them for those choices; it's simply the nature of our industry, where to survive is to look youthful and perpetuate the ridiculous idea that somehow you've managed to stop time and will look twenty-five forever.

In 2000, I had gained weight. It wasn't a lot of weight. It was fifteen pounds, and like most weight gain, it was the product of other things going on in my life. I was accepting that my marriage had failed. I was still decompressing from living in South Africa for three months and what I had witnessed there. I was in a tough spot, so I ate a lot of comfort food and gained fifteen pounds in the process. I remember weighing myself after my clothes stopped fitting and thinking, "How on earth did this happen?"

Immediately, I felt a lot of pressure to lose the weight. As an actress, part of your job is maintaining a certain physical image. I had seen this kind of stress take over many women's lives in the industry; the weight stress that leads young actresses to starve themselves to the point where they can't remember their dialogue because they're so malnourished. I absolutely knew that this wasn't the healthy way to approach my desire to lose the weight. I also knew that I wasn't eating just because I liked food. While I *love* food and have always loved food, I knew that that love was not what drove me to overeat. I was eating to soothe my aching.

I decided the only way out was in. I went into therapy, soul searched, and dealt with all the issues inside that had been suppressed. I enrolled myself in a yoga class and decided ultimately to just be kind to myself and give myself time to heal. Instead of eating, I focused on taking care of myself and exercising. I didn't lose the weight overnight, but eventually it did come off.

In the distraught state I was in before I embarked on my major soul overhaul, if someone had offered me a miracle pill that was guaranteed to melt the weight off of me, I would probably have taken it. If someone had told me that I wouldn't ever act again without engaging in some kind of weight enhancement, I would have thought long and hard about it. I'm not saying that I would have done it, but it definitely would have been a tough decision. I was in a tough place in my life, and the thought that I would lose the only livelihood I've ever known might have been enough to push me to make the wrong choice. Frustration can make people do and think strange things; I'd been acting my whole life, and I wasn't ready to throw in the towel over a few extra pounds. Though I worked off the pounds the hard way, we're in an era when everyone's first reaction is to look for the quick fix that will slow down the hands of time. We are in an era when natural ability just isn't good enough.

This applies to athletes as well. Maybe weight gain is their issue, or maybe it's speed. Maybe they've lost a step on their jump in center field, or maybe they can't steal second anymore. They want to keep their career going and continue to do the one thing they've been doing their whole life. They get older, their bodies don't hold up as well as they once did to a 162-game season, and they look for ways to stay young. They're looking to recover faster, perform better, and get just a couple more hits a week. They go through their numbers from a couple years earlier, they see the downward trajectory of their batting average, they realize that their contract is up for renewal at the end of next season, and they have to make some very difficult choices about what to do. They may not be ready to hang up their spikes yet, but if they don't start to improve, it won't be their decision to make.

So you see the psychologies behind what leads an actress to get plastic surgery and a ballplayer to choose steroids really aren't that different. The big difference between injecting Botox and with taking human growth hormone is that there are no rules against Botox. Now don't get me wrong, I'm not saying that because Botox is considered okay, HGH should be as well. Nor am I condemning anyone who chooses to alter her appearance in the name of age. The reality is more complicated than that, and this is why I think it's important for people to consider the situation before they cast stones. People should understand that elsewhere in society, we encounter decisions similar to those that athletes do. We just don't think about it in those terms. Regardless of what's in the needle, it's all a symptom of the underlying pressure to retain the resiliency of youth.

In the end, it's the so-called innocence of the sport that causes people to hold athletes to a different standard (I guess people gave up on actresses' innocence a long time ago). Ever since the recent steroid scandal began to take hold of professional baseball, people of all manner—baseball fans, people who never watched a game, and congressmen—have been relishing talk about the good old days, a time when the game was "pure." A time when all a baseball man cared about was hitting, fielding, and throwing. No one was looking for money, no one was looking for an edge—these were things that either you had or you didn't. Nine innings, ninety feet from third base to home, nine men on the field, were supposedly all that mattered in these sepia-toned games of old.

Well, I hate to break it to you and to the purists, but I've talked to enough ballplayers and managers to know that, whether it was amphetamines, cocaine, amino acids, or stealing signs, the game hasn't been pure for a long, long time. Players, coaches, and owners have long been looking for an edge, and this is where knowing the pastime's past time becomes so important.

For its first fifty years or so, baseball wasn't just a sport, it was the only sport. While it attracted some class-act talent, it also attracted all manner of riffraff (that's right, I said riffraff) and questionable characters who wouldn't think twice about taking a guy out at second if it meant that that guy wouldn't be able to play in game two of the doubleheader. It was expected that teams would do what they needed to do in order to win. Managers were renowned not just for their pitching changes but for their Machiavellian leadership. Back in those days it was a lot harder to prove that cheating had taken place, so you'd better believe that players did a whole lot more of it. It was just the nature of the game.

Take for instance the most infamous cheating scandal in the history of baseball and perhaps all of sport, which didn't involve drugs or needles—just some mobsters and most likely several drops of booze.

The 1919 Chicago White Sox where the best team in the majors at the time, and the World Series against the Cincinnati Reds was expected to be a rout. But things weren't that simple. Fed up with mismanagement and poor labor relations within the White Sox organization, first baseman Chick Gandil enlisted the help of seven other players to go in on a gambling fix of the World Series, supposedly with the help of organized crime.

Right-handed pitcher Eddie Cicotte, a 29-game winner that year, and Claude "Lefty" Williams, a 23-game winner, were the starting pitchers. Outfielder Oscar "Happy" Felsch and shortstop Charles "Swede" Risberg were on board. (Seriously, I do think nicknames were better back then.) Third baseman Buck Weaver was invited to join the fix but reportedly refused. Weaver was still banned with the others because of his knowledge of the fix and failure to report it. Utility infielder Fred McMullin was not initially invited, or even needed, in the fix, but when he found out about it, he threatened to go public unless he was included. And we all know about outfielder Shoeless Joe Jackson. His participation in the fix is a topic of controversy and debate, not least because he hit .375 during the Series.

Rumors of a fix were immediate, surfacing after the White Sox lost Game 1, 9–1. Manager Kid Gleason reported his concerns to owner Charles Comiskey, and Comiskey went to NL president John Heydler and AL president Ban Johnson. The concerns were dismissed. White Sox secretary Harry Grabiner called Heydler after Chicago lost Game 2, 4–2, but he too was ignored. In the end, the White Sox lost the Series, and the momentum of rumor inspired a grand jury investigation in September 1920. Cicotte and Jackson confessed, but when their confessions were lost, they changed their tune and denied participation. Other key evidence went missing, and the grand jury acquitted them in 1921.

But Kenesaw Mountain Landis wasn't so forgiving. Baseball owners appointed the federal judge to be the first commissioner of baseball, and the day after the players were acquitted, Landis delivered his own verdict: exile. All eight ballplayers were banished from the game forever. Baseball, and the country, healed. Landis saw to it. George Herman "Babe" Ruth helped. Used primarily as a pitcher for the Boston Red Sox, Ruth was traded to the Yankees in 1920, one year after the Black Sox scandal brought the sport to its knees, and his subsequent conversion to an everyday hitter was the ringing bell of a new era for the sport. The timing of Ruth's arrival couldn't have been more perfect for the game. The twenties were huge, and so was Babe Ruth, living large and hitting big for the biggest team in the best nation's biggest game. Long live the home run.

And thus began the new era of innocence, which wasn't so innocent either.

The first and most pernicious illegal substance: spit. Ah, saliva. Not exactly a charming substance, but boy does it do wonders to the movement of a baseball. The spitball has been around forever, and it's probably impossible to credit any one pitcher with inventing it. It was outlawed in 1920 (grandfathering seventeen pitchers who were allowed to throw it until they retired), but that didn't stop pitchers throughout the ages from trying to get away with it. Basically, a spitball is a pitch in which the surface of the ball has been altered by a foreign substance—Vaseline, sandpaper, and, yes, spit.

Joe Niekro, a pitcher for the Minnesota Twins, was suspended in 1987 after being caught with a nail file in his back pocket during a game. A week later, Phillies pitcher Kevin Gross was suspended after umpires found sandpaper in his glove.

Edwin "Preacher" Roe, an All-Star left-handed pitcher

for the Brooklyn Dodgers in the 1940s and '50s, was reported to be an effective spitballer, as was Gaylord Perry, a right-hander who went to the extent of writing an autobiography entitled *Me and the Spitter* in 1974. He was elected into the Hall of Fame in 1991. Go figure.

Wild Pitch — Dirty Business

While the Ray Chapman beaning took dirty balls out of circulation, muddying them up is now not only allowed, but is part of baseball. Brand-new balls, fresh off the factory line, have a slick gloss to them. Pitchers always did what they could to grip the ball, but the best substances were illegal. Beginning in the 1930s, Philadelphia Athletics third-base coach Lena Blackburne helped his pitching staff by harvesting some mud from the Delaware River, near his home in Palmyra, New Jersey. It seemed to work. The Army Corps of Engineers found that the mud possessed a high content of feldspar, which was fine enough to take the gloss off the ball without damaging or discoloring the surface of the ball.

I always thought this story inspired the 1942 film *It Happens Every Spring*, directed by Lloyd Bacon and featuring Ray Milland. The movie is about a college professor, played by Milland, whose experiment is destroyed by a baseball that crashes through his laboratory window. The baseball is covered in the prof's experimental fluid, which, the professor finds, repels wood, and *eureka!* The professor makes more of this magic potion, tries out for the St. Louis Cardinals, who always need pitching, makes the team, and leads them to World Series victory.

I love it. Screenplays were so simple back then and completely entertaining. Don't get me wrong, I love the complexities of *Crash,* but sometimes all you need is a good trigger, and the next thing you know, the protagonist is winning the World Series.

Back to the "magic mud" (as it's now called). It's official name is "Lena Blackburne Baseball Rubbing Mud" (the company describes it as "resembling a cross between chocolate pudding and whipped cold cream"), and buckets of it are shipped to every major- and minor-league team in the nation every spring. Balls are rubbed in it before every game.

The location of Blackburne's Jersey fresh mud farm has been kept secret by the Blackburne family.

★

Some fans yearn for what they consider the simpler, kinder days of the spitter. It was cheating, sure, but it wasn't as *terrible* as steroids. It wasn't as *bad* as drugs. But wasn't it? Didn't it still represent subterfuge and deceit? Didn't it still rely on something other than sheer effort and excellence to win games? To answer that question, consider another artifact of those "simpler" times, one of the most important incidents of cheating in the history of baseball, which until recently was celebrated as an example of heroism, one of the pinnacle moments in the American century.

Men of a certain age will get all trembly and misty-eyed if you ever utter the words "Bobby Thomson." That would be the New York Giants outfielder who hit a walk-off home run off Dodgers pitcher Ralph Branca to win the National League pennant on October 3, 1951. It became known as "the Shot Heard Round the World" and inspired one of the greatest sportswriters of all time to write, "Now it is done. Now the story ends. And there is no way to tell it. The art of fiction is dead. Reality has strangled invention. Only the utterly impossible, the inexpressibly fantastic, can ever be plausible again."

Heartwarming words, but as it turns out, they were written by a sucker. (Sorry, Red Smith.) It wasn't until a *Wall Street Journal* reporter named Joshua Prager wrote about the same event in a book in 2006 that the truth was revealed. The Giants were stealing pitching signs and had been doing so for half a season. Thomson knew what Branca was about to throw before he threw it. The cheaters won.

But somehow saying the cheaters won doesn't quite cut it on this one. It's not so much that the cheaters simply won; in this instance, the cheaters gave baseball and America a defining moment. For many the Shot Heard Round the World became a towering icon of the twentieth century—an event like the assassination of JFK or the moon landing, that everyone remembered where they were when it happened. It has been written about by novelists and historians alike, revisited countless times by those who were there and those who weren't. Cheating created one of the crowning moments of the modern era, and while it's possible that Thomson would have hit that home run anyway, knowing the signs made it a hell of a lot easier.

The Giants' victory and Perry's spitter would all seem to suggest that it's not how you play the game that counts, or even whether you win or lose. What counts is whether you're caught, and then, what happens when all the evidence is examined. Consider George Brett.

The Kansas City Royals were good once, and third baseman George Brett was the leader of the pack. On July 24, 1983, in a close game against the Yankees, Brett stepped in against Goose Gossage, both of whom are now in the Hall of Fame, in the top of the ninth. Brett took Gossage deep for a two-run homer, putting the Royals up, 5–4. Yankees manager Billy Martin quickly met with the umpires at home plate, complaining that the bat Brett used had pine tar far above the allowed eighteen inches. The umpires agreed, called Brett out, and didn't count the home run, and Brett stormed out of the dugout in a fury. He was so upset that he had to be restrained by just about, oh, everyone. You've seen the video, I'm sure. The Royals protested the game, the umpires were overruled, Brett's home run stood, and the game was continued later in the season, picking up after Brett's home run.

In the Brett case, it seems the right call was made. The pine tar was a smidgen too high up on the bat? Did it really affect Brett's performance? No.

In other instances, calls were, well, blown. Take corked bats.

In 2003, alleged steroid user Sammy Sosa was caught using a corked bat when it shattered on a ground ball. He said he occasionally used corked bats during batting practice to give the fans a show. He said that bat must have accidentally gotten mixed up with his game bats. He was suspended seven games.

And then there's Albert Belle. On July 15, 1994, umpires confiscated one of the Cleveland Indians slugger's bats after the White Sox voiced suspicion that it was corked. The Indians knew it was corked, and during the game, relief pitcher Jason Grimsley (who was later the target of a federal-performance-enhancing drug raid in 2006) crawled through the air-conditioning ducts of Comiskey Park, found Belle's bat in the umpires' locker room, and replaced it with another. Problem was, Grimsley replaced it with an autographed Paul Sorrento model. Oops.

Belle was suspended seven games.

Did he learn his lesson? As Belle's former teammate Omar Vizquel wrote in his 2003 autobiography *Omar!*, "all of Albert's bats were corked."

Graig Nettles was suspended ten games for using a corked bat in 1974. Howard Johnson's bats were confiscated throughout his career, though nothing incriminating was ever found.

Greenies, or amphetamines, have reportedly been in the game since the 1940s. They fight fatigue, aid alertness, and basically give the player enough pep to stay in the lineup. I don't sympathize with tired athletes, but I can see how 162 games during the summer heat can wear on a fella. Since 2005, baseball has been more stringent in eliminating amphetamines, and I think the result will be younger teams winning divisions and postseason titles, like the 2008 Rays, the 2007 Rockies, and the 2003 Marlins.

It was only after all the greenies, the stolen signs, the corked bats, and the spit that the current era of swollen necks and bulging home run totals was ushered in. That's how we ended up with the Mitchell Report. So much for baseball's innocence.

I'm not saying we should welcome cheating or cheaters. I'm not saying we should accept it and condone it. But enough with the white-hot rage because people in a high-stakes, big-money game look for an edge, and in so doing, sometimes go over it. Punish them, yes. Make it more difficult to cheat, definitely. But spare the puritan apoplexy.

What's crazy is not that athletes occasionally cheat, or that we're displeased and disappointed. What's crazy is the scale of emotions we feel. Ralph Branca spent his life in ignominy because of the Shot Heard Round the World, and to utter the words "Bobby Thomson" was to invoke godliness. As it turns out, Branca wasn't a bum, and Thomson was not quite as heroic as everyone thought. But is Branca a hero now? Is Thomson a contemptible scoundrel? No. They're men who got caught up in something.

The same is true for our contemporary brand of cheaters. They're men who got caught up in something. Sure they made choices that were wrong for them and the game, but so have countless others throughout the years.

It's hard to understand the distinctions that contemporary critics make between what's happening today and what happened in the past. To me, just about the only difference between now and then is that today's cheating is happening off the field. It's happening in locker rooms and bathroom stalls instead of on the base paths and the pitcher's mound. Personally, I can't figure out how anyone can say that one form of cheating is "better" than another. Can't we just say that they're all bad rather than trying to find ways to show that the past was full of decency and the present is full of deception?

I'm a big believer in individual responsibility. Baseball cheaters should be punished. Punished, yes, but not destroyed. It was true when Shoeless Joe Jackson and the rest of the Black Sox disappointed a nation, and it's true now, for the guys looking for an edge by using the needle.

The real problem with steroids is that the baseball commissioner, Bud Selig, and the Major League Baseball Players Association didn't nip it in the bud (no pun intended) early on. For years both sides opposed testing with little sense of the toll that this position would take on the game. Their negligence turned a problem into an epidemic, leaving an entire era of stats in question. Home runs, hits, and attendance were up, and that meant more money for teams and the league, which meant more money for players, which meant more money for the union. Take all those financial incentives together, and suddenly no one is in a hurry to regulate anything. Enter the puritanical outrage in the form of pundits, grand jury investigations, and Congress.

In March 2006, Selig asked former Senate majority leader George Mitchell to investigate allegations of steroid abuse in major-league baseball. After a year and a half of investigation, the report was finally released in December 2007, naming eighty-nine baseball players who supposedly used steroids or drugs. I believe the Mitchell Report was pointless and a waste of taxpayers' money. If you can't name absolutely everybody, why name the few people it did? Not to mention the fact that much of the evidence implicating these ballplayers was simply hearsay. Some people named names and some people didn't. Hardly factual proof, but it's still enough to stain anyone's career.

Now, I know there are clearly people on that list who used steroids, who deserved to be outed and all that. But in my mind the risks of an endeavor like the Mitchell Report outweigh the benefits. If bringing all this to light means that five of the eighty-nine players are unfairly accused, does that make it worth it? Let's be honest, most of us probably could have figured out who was juicing just by looking at the photos on their baseball cards. No report necessary. I could tell by their necks, their jawlines, their potholed skin. Not to mention the crazy popeye muscles.

Perhaps the worst part about the Mitchell Report is that I'm sure there are plenty of others who got away with it—guys who had juiced for a couple of years, who got their drugs through other channels that the investigators didn't find out about. In a witch hunt you're never going to catch *everyone,* so why name some guys and crucify them, while others get off the hook?

Barry Bonds is undoubtedly one of the greatest players ever. You know what? I didn't have as much of a problem with the idea of him cheating as I did with the possibility that he lied about it. Despite all the controversy and attention, Bonds never admitted any wrongdoing. In contrast, there are guys like Jason Giambi and Andy Pettitte, who simply came clean (inasmuch as Giambi could without violating the terms of his contract). And I totally respect their honesty. Yes, Giambi may have made some bad choices throughout his career, but I must admit, as a purist fan of baseball, I had a newfound respect for the man after he told the truth. If Bonds had said, "I did this because I wanted to be the best and I felt everyone else had an edge because they were using as well. I made the wrong choice. I apologize," I would have forgiven him. I have compassion for anyone trying to do the right thing, anyone who may have had a slip of judgment and then recognized his or her mistakes.

Maybe my biggest frustration with this issue is that Major League Baseball and the players union have yet to own up to their role in all this. A grand jury, a congressional committee, a tell-all book, and they have yet to apologize for their complacency, which had a key role in this off-field drama. Before MLB can solve this issue it needs to recognize the problem and apologize for it. If any employee of any major entertainment corporation were to act inappropriately and offend or alienate his or her audience, the CEO would apologize on behalf of the company. Why is it so hard for Bud Selig to say, "I apologize for the steroid era. We made a mistake with our complacency, and we are taking the appropriate measures to make sure the future game of baseball is played with dignity and integrity."

And here's what I think should happen to the steroid users: Those mentioned in the report (and even those not mentioned) should be given the chance to own up to using steroids and HGH. They should be given amnesty and the opportunity to apologize for what they did. The new, more scrutinizing regulations that were put in place to monitor steroid use should be followed strictly, with every intent to correct the missteps of the past.

The fans, the players, the coaches—everyone should close the book on this latest chapter in the game's cheating history. That's not to say that the steroid-abuse problem is solved, but that we need to stop being outraged by it. As the latest in a long history of cheating episodes, it's our obligation to give it the attention it deserves and then move on. We owe it to ourselves and we owe it to the game.

chapter nine

If I Were Commissioner for a Day (or Three)

Baseball is too much of a sport to be called a business, and too much a business to be called a sport.

—Philip Wrigley

*a*s you've probably figured out by now, I love baseball, but for all that I love it, I recognize that the sport these days is far from perfect. There are a few things I'd change if I could—not because they're awful or they make the game awful, but because I think they potentially get in the way of enjoying it. These are the kinds of changes I would make if I were running the show. (Note to Bud Selig: I do not want your job, but an open invitation to every game is a pretty irresistible perk, so watch your back.)

If I were commissioner, there are a lot of little things that I would tinker with, but of all my gripes, I'd have to say that my biggest is with beach balls. That's why, if I were commissioner for a day, I would ban them.

Now, I know you're most likely wondering what the hell I'm talking about, and why, with all the other issues that this game has, I'm making the innocent little beach balls the target of my aggression. To explain my rationale for this, I have to start somewhere entirely different, with a complaint that many other people have: The game has become too corporate these days. Big companies seem to own everything in the sport, from the ballparks to the replay monitor in center field. For a lot of reasons, baseball today is much more corporate than it used to be. Taking an unscientific survey of myself, I would say that 95 percent of my problems with baseball come from the fact that money is a much more active and obtrusive part of the game.

Simply put, it gets in the way sometimes.

Most fans have complained about this at one time or another; it's a pretty universal problem. But perhaps the complaint is so universal because it's actually true. Baseball is not priced for the fans these days, it's priced for the sponsors. Everything is sponsored, everyone answers to a corporation, and no one wants to take the responsibility of a risk. It's not a cigar-chomping irascible rascal who's calling the shots, but a boardroom of suits that conform to their out-of-touch ideology of pop culture. There was a time when sports pages carried stories about slumps and streaks, pinch-hits and pop-ups. Now there are series about tax-supported sky-boxes, luxury taxes, and how if a conglomerate doesn't get a concession from the city regarding construction of some new luxury seats and this and that, it's moving to a different city.

It sadly seems like it's all about building equity, real estate, saving money, advertising, protecting shareholders, and all that other stuff that has as much to do with baseball—in my mind—as any major corporation has to do with making a good movie or television show. Everything seems to be about avoiding risk. Few people are willing to take a real gamble that a club or a city can turn itself around on its own. But that's the way the world works now. Walter O'Malley might have been a villain to my dad for taking the Dodgers from Brooklyn to Los Angeles, but he took a chance.

This aversion to risk holds true not just in baseball, but in all corporate entertainment. When's the last time a baseball owner—or a film executive, or a television bigwig—took a real chance? In Hollywood, where big corporations like GE and Viacom seem to own all manner of entertainment, they can't find a way to take risks on creativity because they're afraid of the money involved. Similarly these days, when stadiums are named AT&T and PETCO and when it seems like owners care more about spreadsheets than win-loss records, people aren't taking chances; they are merely avoiding risk so they don't lose money and sponsorships. How can we win just enough to keep fans in the seats and the sponsors in the game without paying too much money (unless you're the Yankees)?

The same factors stifle risk taking in my business. How can we put a bankable star together with a decent director and an average writer to produce a movie that will be utterly average but will guarantee us the return we need? It's thinking like this that leads to so much of Hollywood's output seeming utterly the same. It's because it is the same. No one wants to bet on anything unique. It feels like every decision made in *every* aspect of entertainment, whether it is the business of sports, the television business, or the music industry, seems to come from a place of economic fear.

But here's the thing I really don't get: When a city agrees to build one of these new ballparks for the team, aren't taxpayer dollars contributing to that park? How can you then raise the ticket prices when it's our money that makes the new park possible in the first place? It would be one thing if having all these sponsors meant that ticket and concession prices went lower, but somehow the opposite happens. Sometimes it seems like the more sponsors you get, the higher prices are, and that's where this whole notion of corporate baseball really starts to get in the way of the fans' enjoyment of the games.

According to legend, once upon a time, in a galaxy far far away, a woman could go to a ballgame with her husband and kids, get some hot dogs and sodas and a scorecard, and make it home without taking out a second mortgage on her house. I say "legend" because it's hard to believe those days ever existed. If you're reading this, then presumably you're at least a little bit of a baseball fan, and if you're a little bit of a baseball fan, then you've probably attended at least one game at your hometown stadium. Let me ask this quietly, and gently: Can you believe the prices! And they just keep going up every year. Maybe if they didn't raise ticket prices every single freaking year, these parks wouldn't need to have gimmicky attractions. The game itself would give us our money's worth of entertainment.

I can't help but wonder how escalating ticket prices will impact future generations of baseball. I just don't see how, when they can get highlights in real time and watch a game in high-def with a crystal-clear picture, families of four can justify the expense of getting to a game.

And I get it. It's a business. But baseball has to mitigate somehow the insane spiraling of costs for so many reasons.

Wild Pitch — It Sounded Like a Good Idea at the Time—Part I

Believe it or not, there was a time when attendance was so low that ballclubs were willing to do just about anything to try and bring in fans. One-Dollar Hot Dog Night? Yes, please. T-Shirt Day? I'm there. Umbrella Night? Here's my ticket. However, there is one story that proves there is such a thing as the ballpark being too affordable. A little phenomenon that popped up once, known as 10-Cent Beer Night.

Now I'm not sure who could possibly think that was a good idea, but someone did. In May 1974, the Indians were struggling to draw any fans, much like the Tampa Bay Rays of 2008, except that the Indians sucked. They played better than .500 ball precisely once between 1967 and 1975 (in 1968, 86–75). Every year in between, they were a forgettable joke. But the fans weren't laughing. Eighty-five percent of seats at home games, played at the spacious Municipal Stadium (capacity 74,400), went unsold. Yes, some PR genius must have thought, perhaps a happy hour could get bodies into those seats.

So on June 4, 1974, the dime beer promotion drew 25,134 fans (or at least people in the Cleveland area). Problem was, there was no system in place to regulate the amount of beer a person could purchase and consume, or to verify alone if people were of legal drinking age. Nor did the Indians request additional security.

It probably didn't help that the Texas Rangers were in town six days after the two teams met in Arlington, where an on-field fight broke out between them. The Indians lost that game, and animosity influenced the fans before the beers did.

Needless to say, as the game got under way, fans were restless. Firecrackers went off in the upper deck, the smoke of which mingled with the mari-juana fumes of the lower deck. One by one, emboldened fans ran onto the field, either attempting to kiss a player or umpire, sliding into bases, or pulling their pants down for close inspection by Rangers fielders. Indians fans know about the drum corps who sat in the outfield nosebleed section, banging their tribal drums, but on this night, mixed with the firecrackers, beer, and mayhem, the drums marked the pace of a motivated militia.

In the fourth inning, Rangers pitcher Fergie Jenkins took a comebacker in the gut, and the fans cried with derisive approval. And later that inning, when the umps didn't make the call at third that Rangers manager Billy Martin (yes, *that* Billy Martin) wanted, he got the crowd fired up by blowing kisses to them after arguing with the ump.

Bullpens were evacuated at one point during the game when firecrackers rained down. Fans began rushing the field again, this time not one by one, but en masse, stripping off their clothes and attempting to remove the padding on the outfield walls.

When the Indians mounted a rally in the bottom of the ninth to tie the score at 5, winning run at second, a fan ran onto the field and stole the cap of the Rangers left fielder. The player turned to retaliate but tripped and went down. Martin, unable to see from his vantage point in the dugout, assumed the worst when his player went down, and gave the go-ahead for his bench to storm the field and take the game back from the fans, which incited more fans to join the fray.

Fans ripped apart the stadium, turned any loose object into a projectile or weapon, and surrounded the team on the field. Some actually produced knives. The Indians emptied their bat rack and stormed the field, essentially becoming a search-and-rescue battalion.

The game, what was left of it, was forfeited to the Rangers. Police eventually arrived; nine fans were arrested. And the league canceled the Indians' remaining three 10-Cent Beer Nights.

★

If I were commissioner for a day, sure I'd listen to all the justifications by the owners of why it is good business to have $300 seats and $5 bottles of water, and I'd nod sagely, and then I'd deliver my commissioner's decree: All stadiums, everywhere, should set aside at least ten thousand affordable seats because, let's be honest, being at a game, experiencing the sights, the sounds, the smells, is what truly makes a diehard fan for life.

I know, I know. The economics of the game are complicated and everything today costs more than it used to and free agency means players are making more and someone's got to pay, and costs are always passed on to the consumer.

As much as I believe in free agency, it's obviously to blame for the escalation in ticket prices. Teams don't just cost more than they did thirty years ago, they cost a *lot* more. I'll spare the age-old flogging of the Yankees for having the highest payroll of any professional sport, but suffice it to say that eleven of the thirty baseball teams in the majors had payrolls of $100 million or more for the 2008 season. Expensive players and big stars have created attendance figures for MLB that are the highest in the leagues' history. With contracts and ticket sales that big, there are winners and losers in the equation. Agents win. Players win. Owners win. The fans? Not so much.

Go to enough games and listen to enough old-timers, male or female, and I promise, you'll hear the following phrases: "when loyalty actually meant something," "back when players took the field for love, not money," and "overpaid bunch of sissies." While this longing for the loyalties of old has some truth to it, it often manages to whitewash the fact that this game has always been about money. What all those old-timers seem to forget is that behind the men playing for love instead of money were the team owners, who, I promise you, paid a *lot* of attention to money.

As frustrating as free agency can be, it's very easy to forget that there was a time when a very small group of men made large piles of money on the backs, bruises, and rotator-cuff injuries of the leagues' players. It wasn't until the 1970s that an arbitrator ruled that teams could not "own" players (thank you, Curt Flood, St. Louis Cardinals center fielder, unsuccessful Supreme Court plaintiff, and pioneer), which ushered in the era of free agency and the pampered superstar. Nowadays you have marginal players signing gazillion-dollar contracts, and great players abandoning the teams, communities, and fans that gave them their first break to go to other teams, just for a few more million.

But the fans' loss is more than just the price tags of everything. For years, people have argued about the emotional toll that free agency has taken on the game as well, and despite my belief that free agency is right, I'd have to agree that it has come at the expense of fan loyalty in general. In the old days, a player stayed with a team his whole career. If you were a Boston fan, you had Yastrzemski. The Cardinals had Stan Musial. The Giants, Willie Mays. I mean, Jackie Robinson retired rather than play for the rival Giants. He was loyal to the team that gave him his shot. He would rather not play at all than betray his team or the Dodgers' fans. Nowadays, when a player's contract is up, oftentimes, he's gone. Which is fair and the American Way and all, but it's not easy on the fans to watch your guy leave.

My favorite Dodger is Russell Martin. I feel like I have invested lots of money and three years of my life watching him grow as a player and leader. If the Dodgers let him go when his contract is up, or trade him, I will be absolutely heartbroken. If he went to play for any of the other teams in the NL I would be even more heartbroken. Sure, I would get over it, just like I eventually got over Paul LoDuca being traded from the Dodgers to the Marlins, but at the time, it felt like a major betrayal. Sadly, we fans have learned to be well versed in getting over it. We should be used to it by now, but somehow that initial sting that one of your players has up and moved across the country never seems to get any easier.

For this reason, I think free agency is also partly responsible for why there aren't more female baseball fans. You remember those ads from a few years ago? The "chicks dig the long ball" ones? Cute, boys. But missing the point. What *this* chick digs is familiar faces, players I know and love. Statistically, women are the most loyal fans of anything. That's why *Grey's Anatomy* does so great. That's why *Desperate Housewives* is such a hit. That's why the film version of *Sex and the City* made so much money. *Charmed,* where I worked from 1998 to 2006, is the longest-running show with female leads in the history of television. Why? Because of that loyal female fan, who grew up watching the show and supported us no matter what we were producing. The studios and networks have figured out that women like dependability and familiarity. And when the networks cater to that demographic, they maintain their audience. Also, women are the majority of consumers, which in turn means the networks can charge more for advertising time.

These fans, who never miss an episode of their favorite shows, are the same women who might get interested in baseball for a season because the team is winning, or because there's an exciting player, or because their boyfriend has tickets, or whatever. And then the player they have chosen to love gets traded. It's enough to turn off even the most diehard fans, but for a woman who's just starting to learn the game it can be downright heartbreaking. (For what it's worth, I also think that this loyalty is why there aren't many women that play fantasy sports. Sure, there are some women that dabble in them, but mostly I think women's loyalties to their own rosters makes it hard for them to find anything fun about wanting players from opposing teams to succeed just to win a fantasy pool.)

In the end, although it might be dispiriting, it's hard to argue the logic behind free agency. After all, if another company offered you a 50 percent pay increase, wouldn't you want the freedom to consider the offer? I know I would. And that's the dilemma that I constantly have as a fan. I know that it's all business—a billion-dollar business at that—but I can't stop myself from being annoyed that this business gets in the way of simply appreciating the game; that, in order to make up for the rapid turnover in rosters, teams try to court fans with perks and attention grabbers at the stadium that have little to do with the game.

Remember Candlestick Park? Long for the magic of Ebbets Field? Or St. Louis's Sportsman's Park? Reflect fondly on the days of community pride, when a team was the embodiment of your city? Those were the days where the game itself was the only actual entertainment at the park. There was no need for things like pools in the outfield or choo-choo trains after home runs. The game was enough. I'm not sure when the need for more stimulus, with bells and whistles and immediate gratification, all started in entertainment. Maybe it was because the fans started demanding other draws, other reasons to show up at the park. Perhaps, but that seems unlikely. What seems more likely to me is that team owners needed to find new ways to raise money, so they turned to the Toyota fan cam and the Verizon base-running competition.

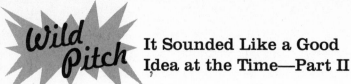

It Sounded Like a Good Idea at the Time—Part II

As much as I hate the corporate sponsorship of everything in baseball, I wish that the White Sox organization could have found a sponsor for this: In 1979, there was another ploy to raise attendance akin to the ill-fated 10-Cent Beer Night, only this time it was at Chicago's Comiskey Park. After a decade of riding the big wave, disco was circling the drain, and to some, Disco Demolition Night probably sounded like a good idea. For haters of the musical genre, this was their last chance to hold disco's head under the water until the last breath escaped, the last air bubble popped, that last and final *bluuup.*

So on July 12, the White Sox hosted the Detroit Tigers for a doubleheader, and in between games, disco's final rites were to be read. Two local radio disc jockeys, who sponsored the promotion, encouraged fans to bring their unwanted disco albums in exchange for a 98-cent admission, representing the radio station's place on the dial (97.9). The records were to be collected and, in between games, placed in a crate and blown up on the field. Yes, you read that right. They were going to bomb disco out of Chicago.

Turns out Chicago residents, not necessarily base-ball fans either, really identified with this promotion. White Sox executives were hoping for an additional 5,000 fans to their regular fan base. Instead, more than 75,000 showed up. Keep in mind that old Comiskey Park seated only about 44,500 fans. Thousands upon thousands of people climbed over the walls and managed to enter the stadium in any way possible, while others were locked out and wandered around the stadium grounds. Television commentators remarked how the fragrance of mari-juana had replaced the smell of hot dogs, peanuts, and Cracker Jacks.

Once the crate was full of records, the promo-tional crew stopped collecting them, but still taken by Disco Demolition Night, fans launched their rec-ords like Frisbees, injuring more fans than was prob-ably reported.

One of the two radio personalities, appropri-ately dressed in camouflage, entered the field, ac-companied by his bombardier—a smoking hot, hardly dressed woman, I assume for show. When he detonated the crate, the fans immediately rushed the field and began pillaging turf, bases, and what-ever else wasn't destroyed by the blast, which by all accounts was more appropriate for invading a small country and a bit much for administering the final blow to disco. Thirty-nine people were arrested, six people reported minor injuries, and calm was eventually restored when Chicago riot police arrived. Umpires ruled a forfeit, but you probably saw that much coming.

★

There are very few ballparks left that still embody the philosophy that the game is enough. We need so much stimulation now in this fast-paced, bigger-is-better society that it has affected how we perceive the whole notion of entertainment. And it's not just the world of sports that has been affected. It's all entertainment.

I grew up listening to albums like *Déjà Vu* by Crosby, Stills, Nash & Young and the Beatles' *White Album*. I still listen to those albums at least once a week, and I listen to them because from beginning to end, I will hear great songs. I can press Play, be transported by the artistry, and then forty minutes later, when the album ends, I am back from a musical journey. Artists of today don't put out great, complete albums anymore. Yeah, maybe there are one or two great songs, but there's no storytelling from track 1 to track 10. I think it's because with the invention of the CD player it became way too easy to just skip to the next track. (Now with iPods forget about it; all bets are off. Insert yet another old-lady joke here.) Before the CD we had turntables and cassettes, and it was far too difficult to lift up that pesky needle and drop it to find the track you wanted to hear or fast-forward to that favorite track, so artists *had* to make great albums from beginning to end.

Any game you are watching should take you on a journey from the first pitch to the last, but all the distractions today get in the way of that journey. It's become almost impossible to get completely engrossed in the actual game itself without something getting in the way. There are so many other things going on to "entertain" the fans. When did baseball become not enough? Which brings me back to beach balls (bear with me—I really am going somewhere with this, I promise).

The beach balls drive me bonkers. Here's how it goes: Someone, somewhere in the stadium, has decided that a full count, one out, runners on first and third, in the late innings of pitchers' duel with a postseason slot hanging in the balance, isn't quite enough excitement, and that it would be a good idea to introduce a beach ball into the environment. So he (or she) throws it. And it bounces around, from one section to the next, no doubt annoying other people like me, who are sending telepathic messages to their favorite batter to please make contact on the next pitch, but delighting lots of other beach ball lovers. And then, —I think it's a law of physics that scientists haven't yet analyzed—the ball, without fail, finds its way to the section where I sit.

And my section mates, these ridiculously polite men and women that I sit near, who *never* chant "Let's go Dodgers" when I'm basically going nuts (they're not really chanters, those folks; I have come to accept that)—these people, who wouldn't chant if their lives depended on it, *love* that freaking beach ball. I don't know why. It's one of life's mysteries, like Steve Sax going all Venusian and not being able to throw to second base in the season of 1983 or why the Florida Marlins insist on dismantling their team after they win a World Series. But they absolutely love the beach ball. Or maybe they don't love it as much as they fear what might happen if they don't embrace the beach ball. Maybe they just don't want to be the elitist rich people who turn the beach ball over to the usher. I don't get it. You're at a baseball game. Do you really need more stimulation than Dodgers versus D-backs, Jeff Kent at the plate, Randy Johnson on the mound? I can't tell you how many times I've been focusing on the game and gotten smacked right in the head by a damned beach ball.

Now I know you might be saying to yourself, "Alyssa, a total overhaul of the economics of baseball just so that people will pay more attention to their team and stop tossing beach balls around? Doesn't that seem a bit extreme?"

No it doesn't (or at least not to me). Because, you see, it's not just the physical act of the beach ball. It's what the beach ball represents. The beach ball is a metaphor that represents all the people for whom baseball simply is not enough. All the people who aren't there for the game, who need some extra reason to go to the ballpark. Okay, okay, maybe I'm being a bit harsh here; after all, you (hopefully not) or your loved ones (hopefully not but possibly) might really enjoy bouncing beach balls during a game. If so, I don't mean to offend, but seriously, you need to snap out of it. If the pitching, hitting, base stealing, home run blasting, manager arguing, dust kicking, home plate colliding, and double play turning aren't enough for you, and instead you need to bounce an inflated, multicolored plastic ball, I think it's time to find another sport.

Oh, and another thing . . . If I were the commissioner for *two* days, I'd change the rules regarding interleague play. First off, I'd make the visiting team the home team. That way, the hometown fans would have a chance to see something we don't ordinarily get to see—our team, in away uniforms, in person. And I'd make the visiting team's league rules apply. So if you're a Chicago Cubs fan, and the Seattle Mariners are visiting, you get to see the designated hitter, in your park. (Commissioner Selig, if you adopt this one, you don't have to give me credit. But it would be nice.)

If I were the commissioner for *three* days I'd abolish the DH. I know all of you American Leaguers just spit out your gum when you read that, but seriously, it's a cop-out position. There was no DH when this game first came about. There was no DH, because they treated all players like they were equal. Pitchers were important, but they still had to be able to swing a bat. I like the complexity of the double switch. I think the DH messes with the equilibrium of the game. Maybe it's because I'm a National League girl, but I believe that pitchers should hit—end of story. There should be no such thing as a free pass, and I'm proud that the National League teams can recognize that.

And . . . please, no instant replay for anything other than a home run or a foul ball. Human judgment and human error are part of the game that I adore.

And . . . the All-Star Game should not determine home-field advantage for the World Series. That should go to whoever has the better record.

Okay. That's it. I'm done now.

chapter ten

All You Need Is gLove

During my youth, love will be my teacher; in my middle age, my help; and in my old age, my delight.

—Kahlil Gibran

Carl Pavano—*Yes*

Tom Glavine—*No*

Barry Zito—*Yes*

Josh Beckett—*God, no (although I do think he is an amazing pitcher)*

Brad Penny—*Yes*

Russell Martin—*No*

Okay, now that we've gotten *that* out of the way, let me preface this by saying, I am friends with almost all my exes that I have had substantial relationships with. Except for one guy who wasn't a ballplayer but was a player nevertheless and just an overall jackass (you know who you are). Carl, Barry, and Brad are amazing guys and I have nothing but respect for them. I really look back on that time of my life with great fondness. I don't have much of a social life, but I do have season tickets for the Dodgers.

Okay. So that period of my life went like this: I was the girl loved by everyone and no one all at once. You must know a girl like this. You can't understand why she is still single. Men adore her, profess their love before the chicken satay arrives; then the phone rings one day, and it's her telling you he left her. Or at least that's what you think she's trying to tell you, but the sobbing makes it hard to decipher the exact phrasing. Then she does that silent cry and you think the phone went dead, or worse, she went dead. Then the ten-second silence is broken by that phlegmy inhale and then more incoherent screeching.

Yeah, that was me, the incoherent screecher.

I say "that *was* me" because, thankfully, I have grown tremendously since then. As I've already mentioned, your twenties are an odd time. You are trying to understand yourself, usually with the help of other people because you'd have no idea where to begin the process on your own. So you get a strange mixture of perspectives and suggestions on how to live your life, some of which work but most of which don't. It's basically a decade when your mantra becomes, as my dad would say, "Well, that didn't work." It really takes time alone to figure yourself out, and only after you've done that can you decide what you need and want from a relationship.

I definitely felt heartache during those breakups. I'll admit it. But that heartache led to growth, great friendships, and a better understanding of the game, so the heartache wasn't all for nothing. Yeah, I dated three baseball players. Not only that, they were all pitchers, imagine that. (But the one in the middle was a lefty, so I don't know if he really counts.) All three were very different men but nevertheless clearly heroes in the eyes of a girl who idolizes baseball players. I am not a total dolt. I saw that I was repeating a pattern that had to be broken. Each lasted seven months too: further proof of a definite pattern.

To be completely honest, after Barry and I broke up I swore off baseball players. But then one night in 2005, I was down in the Dugout Club after a Dodgers game, waiting for the stadium traffic to die down before getting in the car for my trek home, and Brad came in. I had met him before when he played for the Marlins in 2003. We sat and reconnected and talked. Before I knew it, three hours had passed and it was 1 A.M. We cleared the place out. He then looked at me and said, "Let's go down to the clubhouse." Well, that was just about the best invitation I had ever received.

The clubhouse? Are you kidding me? Mind you, this was before my partnership with MLB for the clothing line and before I did my postseason commentary for TBS. I had never been in a clubhouse before.

I walked in and heard the melody of a thousand voices

singing some kind of religious chant. I was like a little girl walking into a magical castle with unicorns and fairies all fluttering about. It was a lot smaller than I had thought it would be, and I thought how small it must feel when the whole roster is in there getting ready for a game.

"Put this on," he said while handing me his jersey and a batting helmet. Oh, dear God. I put on his jersey, which came down past my knees.

"Does this come in a petite?" I asked. And I put on the helmet. It bobbled with even the slightest move of my head.

"Come with me," he said with that charming southern twang he has going on. I followed him, and we ended up right in front of the batting cage.

"Oh my God. Is this the batting cage Kirk Gibson used to warm up on *that* night?" I shamelessly asked.

"Yes, ma'am. Come in with me." I walked into the batting cage, bobble helmet and all, and then I heard voices approaching. I thought to myself, "Oh shit, we are going to get in trouble." As the voices got closer, I could see the faces the voices belonged to. Eric Gagne and Jason Repko were coming in for a peek at all the commotion.

"Repko, catch for me," Brad demanded.

"Are you crazy? With no gear on?" Repko said. What a wimp.

"I won't throw hard," Brad replied.

Repko grabbed a glove and entered the cage.

"Stand right here," Brad told me while handing me a bat. "Choke up a bit." I did.

"Brad, what are you doing?" Repko asked, not hiding his smirk very well.

"Okay. Are you ready?" Brad said to me, and then before I could answer he went through a truncated version of his windup and blew the ball right past me. Gagne started laughing hysterically.

"Fuck off," I said.

"I thought you weren't going to throw hard?" Repko asked. I couldn't believe what was happening then, and as I am writing this now, I still can't believe it happened.

"Okay. I wasn't ready before, tough guy. I'm ready now. Bring it," I taunted. Big Mistake. Big. Freaking. Mistake. He blew the ball past me again. At least I swung that time. Shit. I'm down 0–2. Gagne with his damn laughing, Repko, Brad, Kirk Gibson, big helmet. It was all too much for me to bear.

"He will not strike me out," I chanted in my head. "He will not strike me out." And he went into his windup again. He released the ball and then out of nowhere I heard the word "swing" from the peanut gallery (Gagne) and I swung. Boy, did I swing. I hit that ball so hard. It flew. The contact made that great line-drive noise. It almost took Brad's head off too.

"Jesus," said Brad.

"Good girl," said Gagne, like a proud batting coach. I felt like such a badass.

So, yeah, Brad had me at "Let's go down to the clubhouse."

But that was exactly the problem. I remember having a conversation with my therapist in 2005 when Brad broke up with me (in L.A. we all have therapists). My therapist said that I was giving my basic, superficial needs too much power.

All of those men were attractive to only one part of me, that part being my ego. I wasn't listening to the rest of my being. My ego loved baseball players because of this idealistic hero worship thing that I had going on, but the rest of me needed more. It wasn't until I was alone and unattached for an extended period of time that what my therapist said really resonated.

My ex-husband was attractive to a whole other part of me, but the attraction was just as one-sided. He was this deep, dark enigma that awakened me creatively and artistically. Everything was so heavy and yet ethereal with him. Don't get me wrong—it was inspiring, and he is an extraordinary person that I will always love dearly, but there were often times (mostly while listening to Mazzy Star) when I could almost hear my ego yawning. So what did I do? After my eleven-month marriage, I went for men that were the polar opposite of my ex-husband. I went for men that the other deprived side, my ego, responded to.

It makes so much sense to me now. Duh. But it took me a long time to be able to integrate these observations into my life. There was a lot of saying, "Well, that didn't work."

A food analogy for you (I am Italian after all). My favorite food is ice cream (mint chocolate chip to be exact), but if I had to eat it every day it wouldn't be my favorite anymore. Pitchers are my ice cream. I ate ice cream for almost two years collectively if you include the lefty. That also explains the weight gain. It was time for some broccoli. Sure, it's not as tasty, but it's better for your health. I am now with a man that is on the same page as I am concerning politics, morals, human behavior; he's not famous, he loves baseball as much as I do . . . and for dessert . . . he has a great arm.

As I moved on from ballplayers and looked closely at the choices I made, one of the conclusions I came to was that the most important thing for me was finding someone that I had common interests with, someone who shared my passions. I wanted someone I could enjoy a baseball game with, and that's not so easy when the person you're dating is actually in the game you're watching. So much of what I love about this game is being able to enjoy it with others. There's nothing better than watching a baseball game with loved ones—be they significant other, family, or friends. Nothing. You can yell at the umps together, laugh when your brother says, "Way to go, Snacks," and sway as one during the seventh-inning stretch.

 **Rounding Third**

Philandering baseball players are nothing new. But when Wade Boggs admitted his four-year affair with Margo Adams, we finally had the face for a term we'd only heard a few times: sex addict. At that moment, Wade Boggs and his wife, Debbie, became the Bill and Hillary of the baseball world. It was nothing if not comically awkward.

Adams told her side of the story to anyone who would listen, such as Phil Donahue, *Penthouse,* and people who came out to see her during an eight-city publicity tour. Naturally, Boggs's and Adams's stories differed. He admitted to being a sex addict and said the affair lasted two years, taking two years to get out; she said it lasted four years and everyone in the Red Sox organization knew about it, allowing her to fly with the team when they took to the road. Speaking of the road, Kansas City fans wore Margo masks when Boggs came to town.

In the end, Adams filed a $6 million palimony suit, which was raised to $12 million, and the Hall of Famer settled out of court for an undisclosed amount. Through it all, Mrs. Boggs stayed by her husband.

★

In truth, what I was looking for was not that different from what most people are looking for: someone who would respect my enthusiasm for things. One thing that was good about dating ballplayers was that I never had to question whether they were as excited about baseball as I was. As you may know, this can definitely be a difficult hurdle for some people: What if the person you're crazy about isn't so crazy about the game you love?

It doesn't matter if you're a guy or a gal; if you're a fan and if you're dating, you've probably encountered some version of this dilemma. The order of events usually goes something like this:

- You meet someone in March.

- You talk a lot. It turns out that person is pretty cool.

- You spend every waking minute together for an entire month. . . .

Then it happens. Opening day is upon you, and suddenly your schedule fills up in a totally different way. Your nights are cluttered with pizza, you start to check ESPN.com compulsively, and vague chunks of your weekend are devoted to this apparently strange ritual of watching nine men run around a diamond for three hours.

Now I'm not someone who gives a ton of relationship advice, but this is about baseball, so I feel reasonably qualified to throw in my two cents. If that person you met back in March happens to be a fan too, you're all set, but what if that isn't the case? What if the person you're dating is into you but just not that into baseball? Shocking as it may seem, some people don't always find it to be a turn-on when the person they're dating is really into baseball. I've heard stories of male baseball fans who were actually turned *off* after they had conversations about baseball with the girl they were dating. As though their girlfriend knowing something about an amazing sport was somehow a bad thing.

The men I have dated have embraced the fact that I love sports; however, I did once have a disappointing conversation with an actor (who will remain nameless) about baseball. We were working together, and one day while we were having lunch he told me that he was a huge Angels fan. I was elated to hear that he liked baseball and that we had this in common. I went into a soliloquy about the Angels and Mike Scioscia. I went on and on about the roster, the starting rotation, thinking this was a great way for us to connect. I finished strong, and he just looked at me and blinked a couple of times.

"What?" I asked him.

Do you know what his reply was? He said with an absolute, honest straight face: "I feel emasculated."

Good thing we weren't dating, because if we were it would not have been pretty. As it was, I just had to turn the other cheek.

Anyway, whether they feel emasculated or just plain irritable about the game, those kinds of hang-ups and impediments to couples' fandom leave you with the age-old dilemma: how to convert someone to the game—preferably before the All-Star break.

If you've been a baseball fan for any amount of time, you've probably heard the same set of criticisms about the game from nonfans. The list usually includes some combination of the following:

- Baseball is boring.

- Nothing ever happens in baseball. (Note: This is not actually a different criticism from the aforementioned "Baseball is boring"; however, nonfans like to say each of these things as though they were two separate reasons, so I've included them like that here.)

- Innings last too long.

- There are not enough home runs.

- There's not enough scoring.

- I don't get it. What's so great about it?

- I like football. (I'm not really sure how this is a criticism, since science has demonstrated repeatedly that it is quite possible to like multiple sports.)

- I don't understand the rules; therefore, I don't like the game. (Note: This has to be the most irrational reason not to like anything.)

- Why would someone get so worked up about a game in which someone tries to hit a small leather ball with a whittled-down two-by-four. (Note: This is not an actual criticism of the game, but more like the rambling words of a sports-loathing lunatic.)

On their faces, these criticisms are wrong, superficial, uncreative, and totally baseless, but while you might be able to dismiss them when they come from a disgruntled coworker or your next-door neighbor who always swipes your morning paper, it's a lot harder when these words are coming from someone that you love (or even just someone that you like). Hearing any combination of those words can be a deal breaker for some, a hindrance to romance for others. Regardless, it's safe to say that for a fan, it's a pretty big problem.

So how to make sure that baseball becomes important to the people who are really important to you?

Make the Game an Event

When I'm at home, watching the game on TV, I make sure all the speakers in the house are carrying the broadcast. I put out lots of yummy food too, and sometimes I will wear Dodgers gear, including, but not limited to, my lucky jersey. Stock up on packages of baseball cards and hand them out to your guests. My mom still gives my brother and me baseball cards when we watch the games at my parents' house. I don't even know where she keeps them. We'll just be sitting on the couch and she'll hand us a couple of packages each. Also, I find a great way to get people involved is to make a friendly wager on the game. It's amazing how when personal winning or losing is involved people suddenly find passion.

Share

Tell your loved one whatever personal information you may have about your team's roster. Part of what makes watching the Olympics so intriguing is watching the personal stories about the athletes. Insight into the athletes' struggles or odd coin collection or whatever gives us something to identify with or relate to and makes us want to root for them. This is another reason why Vin Scully is the best in the business. The guy has a plethora of random facts about the players that make you feel personally connected to them and want to root for them. He'll say things like "Did you know that Andre Ethier had a pet armadillo growing up? And by the way, the count is one and two."

Don't Forget the Big Picture

At the game, as much as I'm concentrating on the pitch count and where the outfielders are positioned and whether the runner on first has a big lead or not—all the little details that any obsessive fan obsesses about—I'm aware that if I'm trying to get someone interested in the game, I have to take it slow. It took me years of lap sitting and listening before I became a fanatic. Why should anyone else be different? So I remember the big picture. Which is, nachos and pop to make sure no one's hungry or thirsty, a blanket in the early and late season to make sure everyone's warm, a mitt to catch any foul pop flies, and lots of smiles.

Teach Them the History of the Sport

I don't care how uninterested people may be about watching baseball; they can't deny that the history of the game is fascinating.

Remember Your Audience

Do I say, "Baby, baseball allowed me to connect with my family in a way that nothing else ever has"? Do I say, "Baseball reminds me that life is uncertain and unpredictable and that you have to live in the moment?" Do I say, "At a time in my life when I was searching for a professional identity and personal happiness, I found fulfillment in a children's game, played by adults, and it was that very game that saved me"?

Not exactly. What I say is, "Watch where the shortstop positions himself on that deep fly to the gap in left field." I say, "See the way the hitter is shifting his back foot? Watch for the hit-and-run." I say, "Isn't this the life? Don't you just love this?"

That's what my dad did for me. That's what I try to do for others.

Wild Pitch The Most Shocking Trade of All Time

Not all baseball romances end well. Yankees starting pitchers Mike Kekich and Fritz Peterson had been friends since 1969. But Kekich and Peterson took their friendship to the next level when they swapped wives. It started in 1972, when the two *players* went out on a double date with their better halves. I don't know what happened, only what's been reported, but it seems well documented. Apparently, sometime during dinner the couples joked about wife swapping, and by the end of the night the joke reached its punch line when the couples switched beds. Then, during the off-season, Kekich moved in with Mrs. Peterson, and Peterson moved in with Mrs. Kekich, and they got married (to each other) in 1974. The other couple didn't last.

Call me old-fashioned, but I have a hard time believing there isn't some ill will lurking beneath the surface here. In matters of the heart, someone always gets hurt. And listen, I've got a brother, and I know all about boys and their loyalties to each other and how they'll do anything for each other. I get it. Okay? I get it. But the story of Mike and Fritz is just strange.

★

The flip side to all this is that you may be one of the naysayers, one of the people who just don't get baseball and want nothing to do with it. You are a nonfan, but your significant other is not. What do you do then? Do you let baseball get in the way of your feelings? Do you throw in the towel over a 162-game season?

These are all reasonable questions that lead me to a story about my slightly ridiculous crochet habit.

My fiancé doesn't crochet (shocking, right?). Actually, my brother and my fiancé like to team up and call my beautiful granny squares "pot holders." I've been making the same granny-square blanket since the late eighties. Someday I will finish that pot-holder blanket. Anyway, my fiancé hasn't shown any evidence that he's about to subscribe to *Crochet World* ("For all those with crochet in their hearts"), but he knows *I* like to crochet, so he tries. He really tries. In fact, last year when we were in New York he spent two hours in a yarn shop with me in the Village. He kept bringing me different yarn that he liked and really just seemed interested in the whole damn experience. And sometimes he will help me untangle my yarn when there's a massive knot that I can't get out by myself. In those moments, I just want to kiss him.

Along the same lines, I once dated a guy that loved to fish. The whole time I was with him I kept thinking, "How is it possible that one guy could have so many passionate thoughts about peacock bass? It's a fish, for God's sake." He could spend hours talking about tackles, lures, lines, and rods. While that might sound appealing to you fishermen out there, I was definitely not a fishing person. But the situation left me with a choice: I could either try to segue any conversation about fishing into talking about the Dodgers' team batting average (which, believe me, is a lot harder than it sounds), or I could ask him questions about his beloved peacock bass like "Why is it called a peacock bass? Does it have feathers?"

Well, let's just say that I took the latter option. I tried. I really tried.

You get where I am going with this? Your girlfriend has a habit you don't get? You can certainly ignore it and hope it's just a passing phase. Your boyfriend does something you think is a waste of time? You can get whiny and bitch about how it's "me time." Or you can do what I try to do, and what my fiancé does so effortlessly. He sees that I am doing something I love and supports the ridiculous habit, and me.

Which leads me back to baseball. If you're one of the folks who couldn't care less about a no-hitter or a grand slam or a diving catch at the wall, but your boyfriend, or girlfriend, or spouse, or whatever, can't get enough of baseball, at least *act* like you're mildly interested. And be open to the idea that you might be interested someday. The point here isn't how great baseball is, or the way it can open a person's heart, or how it saved my soul (it is, it can, and it did). The point is . . . love.

If you're interested in someone, whether at the lofty level of a soul connection or on a more simple ego level, then you should at least respect what he or she is interested in. Have an open mind. You don't need to suddenly be first in line at the batting cages, or a season ticket holder. You just need to be supportive of your loved one's enthusiasm for the game.

If you really are a baseball fan, the game is a part of your life, and hopefully it's here to stay. If you're in a relationship and the other person is completely unwilling to accommodate your fandom, I'd say you really have to think about this whole thing long term. Now I'm not saying that you need to break up with someone over the game, but if baseball is really getting in the way, chances are there's something else that's not quite right with the relationship.

If you're with a girl who likes the ballet, either you have to have an open mind and enjoy ballet yourself; or, if no matter how hard you try, you can't get the appeal, you must at least respect that your honey sees something beautiful in an arabesque that you don't. Give someone the freedom to have her passions and be exactly who she is. I think it's important for everyone to have passions, for people to do things that bring them happiness.

You never want to be with someone who doesn't respect the things you love. Especially if one of those things happens to be a 4-3-2 double play with one out in the top of the seventh.

chapter eleven

The Off-Season Blues in G

*People ask me what I do in the winter when
there's no baseball. I'll tell you what I do. I stare
out the window and wait for spring.*
—ROGERS HORNSBY

*L*ove and self-forgetting. Villainy and the most underhanded kinds of cheating. Hope, and dreams of triumph, and dashed expectations. They're all there, and they're the reasons that if you're seriously invested in the game and all its glories, you so desperately need the off-season.

These days we need it more than ever. Time was, if you were a fan, even a serious fan, the game was a huge part of your life. But it wasn't your entire life. Not like now. A fan these days can live baseball 24/7 if he or she isn't careful. Can you imagine a time without television? Without cable? Can you envision a universe where you couldn't witness your favorite center fielder's miracle against-the-wall felony robbery of a sure homer late at night on ESPN's *SportsCenter*? Can you imagine more than a few minutes in your car not listening to your local radio jocks letting loose on your team's latest slumping veteran or promising but frustrating rookie outfielder, or cringing at their pure animal savagery as they call for your manager's head? Can you remember a time when, if you were out of town, the only way to check on how your team did the night before was to wait until the next morning, buy a newspaper, and scan the box scores in the sports section?

These days, with around-the-clock highlights on television, scores at the click of a keyboard mouse, and an entire industry devoted to analysis, criticism, and rumormongering, it's easy to forget the days when the only way to see a ball game was in person, and the only way to hear about it was over the radio. (Or so I've heard. I think that world was around at approximately the same time that kids drank egg creams and gobbled ballpark franks in my dad's beloved Brooklyn.) Today a person with a wireless hookup and a computer can watch games an entire season without ever getting close to a ballpark frank, much less a ball game.

One of the things that have always made baseball so pure, and so alluring, is its spaces, vast or intimate. The space between the shortstop and the second baseman, between infielders and outfielders. The yawning gaps in the outfield, the fixed and immutable tunnel between the pitcher's mound and the batter's box. The cozy proximity between umpire and catcher. The elastic but always at least slightly predictable yard or three separating the swift runner on first base from the safety of the bag. The space between the regular season and the postseason, the playoff games and the World Series.

Part of the game's beauty was the space between the fan and the game too. And then that space shrank. *The Game of the Week* begat *Sunday Night Baseball* begat midweek high-lights begat cable packages. Students of box scores became call-in-show junkies became fantasy-league managers. It's hard not to get seduced. Nowadays, not only do I occasionally check how the Dodgers are doing by booting up and logging in, and not only do I surf various sites for tidbits about who's doing what in the Pacific Coast League, the Cape Cod League, and other leagues non–baseball fans have never even heard of, I *blog* about the game.

It's fun. It's exciting and enthralling. And it's exhausting. But without perspective, a fan can get burned out. Baseball is, in many ways, like a boyfriend or spouse. You can love him, you *should* love him, but you need to learn that he exists without you, and you without him. You need to learn the same thing about baseball, that as much as you care, you need to be able to step back.

One way is of giving yourself some distance, paradoxi-cally, to pay even closer attention to the time of year when you're watching a game. Early-season games might seem meaningless, but if you pay attention, you'll notice rookies running out grounders harder than they'll ever again run out grounders in their careers, veterans near the end of their professional lives bearing down for each at bat. T. S. Eliot said that April is the cruelest month, and for those who are given one last chance in the majors and don't make it, it's true. So underneath a gentle spring sky, there's a fierce struggle going on, and if you're a fan who's looking, you can see it. That's enough to give anyone perspective.

Similarly, late in the season, if your team is all but out of the playoffs, what possible interest could a meaningless game with another out-of-it team hold? A lot of interest. Is your manager giving up? Is he in trouble with the head office? Is the guy who was smacking home runs for the Triple-A farm club getting a chance? And what does it say about a player in his last year, with no shot at playoff glory, who stills crashes into walls while trying to help his team? Those are the inspiring answers you get to learn at "meaningless" late-summer games.

If you're a fan, every game means something. Paying attention, then, helps you get closer to the game and its mournful, flinty truths while keeping perspective about them.

The same can be said for the postseason. What I've learned about the playoffs and the Word Series is to be very, very excited. But not *too* excited.

It's not that I don't appreciate the postseason. I do. And it's not that I don't recognize the majesty of St. Louis Cardinal Jack Clark taking Tom Niedenfuer deep in Game 6 of the 1985 National League Championship Series. And it's not that I don't long to see the Dodgers win a World Series again. But the truth is, part of who wins that classic matchup is based on the same factors as who wins a regular-season game—

skill, smart managing, the ability to bounce back, and luck. That's what makes the game great. But the notion that post-season games are somehow more important, or more pressure-packed, or more, I don't know, *special* than a contest in the middle of May, or July, or even April, obscures a larger truth, which is this: *Every* game is special, and it's how a player performs in each game, and in every game, that determines his success, not how he plays in one series.

For years, I had pretty limited postseason experience (quite limited actually), but like so many fans before me, I learned the risks of postseason exuberance the hard way in the fall of 2008. I found myself an adult in a whole new baseball situation as I watched my Dodgers win a postseason series and move on to the NLCS. We hadn't won a postseason series since 1988, when I was just fifteen, but I had always appreciated postseason ball. It was fun to watch the games of the fall even if my heart wasn't emotionally invested in the teams that were playing. I could really just sit back and appreciate the fundamentals at their best.

This fall proved different. I wasn't just invested in who won, I was all in. I sat in my seat with a white-knuckled, sweaty-palmed death grip on whatever I was holding at the time. Every pitch meant something. Every out. Every managerial move. Every call by the ump. The fans were alive. They stood when there were two outs and two strikes, waving those rally towels as if they possessed magical powers to make the batter strike out.

"Throw him the chair!" my brother screamed. Translation: "Sit him down."

The whole event felt so much more intense after the ups and downs we'd had during the season. With their terrific start, Arizona made our division pretty competitive from the beginning, and by the All-Star break, I thought we were in trouble. Torre was doing his best, but we had a lot of unfortunate injuries. And then, just when things seemed a bit bleak, like a gift from God, Manny showed up to shake things up with his bat and his infectious personality. All at once, I realized that one player could make the difference between a good team and a great team.

I know Boston fans have their issues with Manny, and honestly, I probably would too if Manny had done to the Dodgers what he supposedly did to the Red Sox. But everything is relative, and the arrival of Manny brought a new energy to the field, excitement to the stands, and even more important, chemistry to the clubhouse. It was so refreshing to see our roster leaning over the rails for a closer look at the action. He brought new weight to the Dodger franchise in the eyes of the media. The team needed him. The organization needed him. Perhaps most important, the fans needed him. We proudly wore Manny dreadlocked wigs and T-shirts with "Mannywood" written boldly across the chest.

As I am writing this, I don't know if he'll be back on the team in 2009, but I loved watching him and hope I get more opportunity to do so. The bat just looks different in his hands. It didn't matter what pitch he was swinging at—you just knew that no matter where the ball ended up, there was a good chance he could crush it.

As you might expect, losing to the Phillies in the NLCS was devstating. My brother and I were inconsolable. As lame as it might sound, a little piece of my heart broke that night. An even bigger piece of my brother's heart broke that night. The game that we were eliminated in was at Dodger Stadium, and we stayed for about an hour after the last out. In that hour, players came out for curtain calls and blew kisses to the fans that were still there. I would say over a thousand fans stayed, and we were a rowdy bunch. Frank McCourt and his lovely wife stuck around. A chant started. "Please sign Manny." Clap, clap. Clap, clap, clap. "Please sign Manny," the Dodgers fans shouted.

Nomar came out of the dugout, and the crowd erupted in applause and cheers. He waved and put his hand over his heart paying tribute to us fans. He took a long look around, soaking up the moment, his moment. It seemed like he was saying good-bye to the stadium; I hoped he wasn't saying good-bye to baseball.

Tommy Lasorda said a few words into a microphone. He thanked "the best fans in baseball." He finished up his speech by saying, "When you lay your head down on the pillow tonight, say a prayer for Tommy and the Dodgers."

It was a vivid moment, and while we reached a disappointing end, there was something strangely uplifting about the whole scene. As we were walking to the car, I saw daddies holding sleepy kids with their baseball gloves still on, draped over their father's backs. I found solace in the idea that even though we weren't moving on to the World Series, memories were made that night. The children of the fans from '88 had their own stories to tell. A whole new generation of Dodger fans got to experience NLCS baseball for the first time. And who knows, maybe one of these years we'll actually win.

While the postseason weeks in the fall of 2008 were great, they also exposed me to something I hadn't dealt with in a long time: postseason fans. Or fair-weather fans. Or maybe a more accurate way to express my feelings would be to call them what they are: fake fans. Seeing people jump on the bandwagon only to get off at the first stop is every perennial fan's epic frustration. That columnist in your local paper who always counts out your team and finds every reason to speak ill of them? That neighbor who insinuates that they're never going to win the wild card much less their division? The guy who works the graveyard shift at the convenience store and runs his mouth incessantly about how the team batting average is a paltry .270? These are the first people to turn around and start beaming when your team has sealed up the division title with seven games left in the season.

To be honest, there are few emotions that can rival what a true fan feels when witnessing late-season converts like these in action. The only way I can describe it is to say that it's somewhere between satisfied vindication and disgruntled annoyance. As fans, one of the biggest recurring nuisances that we have to deal with is other people talking trash about our team. It's bad enough when the people in rival cities or the guys on *SportsCenter* do it, but when it happens in your own backyard it gets downright aggravating. To then turn around and hear these naysayers praising the same group that they were denigrating two months earlier is at once completely satisfying (because it means you were right all along) and really, *really* upsetting (because it means they're trying to take credit for something they didn't support).

Look, I want everyone to be a fan, and I do recognize that having a good team gets a city or a region excited in a way that a mediocre team does not. At the same time, I think it's important to remember that after the postseason ends—whether your team wins or loses—the hope is that new fans were made. It's fine if people use the postseason as an excuse to get into the game, but they have to stay interested even after the last at bat. The postseason can be terrific for energizing new fans, but they have to realize that this is a bus that you don't get off once you get on.

I want everyone to love baseball the way I love baseball. And if a bunch of hooha about the ineffable wonders of the Fall Classic and the superpowers of Bucky Fucking Dent gets someone to appreciate the game the way I do, great. But it's like those television ads that sell the "hushed majesty" of Georgia during the Masters golf tournament. I have nothing against hushed majesty, nor the country club members at Augusta, where the Masters is played. (Other than them not letting in women. Seriously, guys, what the hell are you thinking?) But aren't respect and affection for golf the reason to love the Masters. And isn't fascination for baseball the reason to love the postseason?

Maybe I'm cranky because the Dodgers lost in the NLCS in 2008. Maybe I'm a little bitter because as much as I love reliving Kirk Gibson's ninth-inning shot and Orel "Bulldog" Hershiser's indomitable grit from that era, I'm ready for some new happy endings to my postseason memories. Anyone for whom postseason success is a distant memory can relate, but that doesn't mean that you give up. You do what we all have to do from time to time: You show up at games, cheer as loudly as possible, and wait it out. If there's anything to be learned from the 2004 Red Sox, it's that like all things, this too shall pass, and when it does, your fans better be ready.

Wild Pitch To Edit, or Not to Edit

In 1979, Garry Templeton was having an All-Star-caliber season as a shortstop, a follow-up to his 1977 All-Star campaign. But he was passed over as a starter for the All-Star Game, which he took as a slight. Hey, to be fair, Templeton had better numbers than big-shot shortstops Larry Bowa and Dave Concepcion. But, alas, he wasn't tabbed to start, at which point Templeton uttered his now famous words, "If I ain't startin', I ain't departin'." Sports desk editors were faced with a dilemma as old as the game. Namely, to edit for slang, or to quote verbatim?

I've always been a fan of the direct, uncleaned-up quote. Can you imagine what Yankees catcher

Yogi Berra would have sounded like had sportswriters decided to make sense of some of his, um, more unusual proclamations? How would they have translated "You better cut the pizza in four pieces because I'm not hungry enough to eat six"? Or, "A nickel isn't worth a dime today"?

And then there was Yankees manager Casey Stengel. The Old Perfessor was a quote waiting to happen. Not necessarily an intelligible quote, but a quote. In fact, so out there were Stengel's utterances that they inspired a new word to describe them: "Stengelese."

When, in 1958, the Yankee skipper was discussing antitrust laws and whether his Yankees would continue their winning ways, he said: "Well, I will tell you I got a little concern yesterday in the first three innings when I saw the three players I had gotten rid of, and I said when I lost nine what am I going to do and when I had a couple of my players I thought so great of that did not do so good up to the sixth inning I was more confused but I finally had to go and call on a young man in Baltimore that we don't own and the Yankees don't own him, and he is doing pretty good, and I would actually have to tell you that I think we are more like a Greta Garbo–type now from success."

What??? Did anyone get that? No, of course not. That was Stengelese at its best. Or worst. His immortal-if-bizarre sentiments, along with Templeton's pungent take on the All-Star Game, stand as reminders that when it comes to famous athletes saying famous (or infamous) things, journalists have a tough job.

As someone who has been quoted correctly before, as well as misquoted and quoted out of context, I can sympathize with players who complain about being misunderstood. Take Gary Sheffield. Sheffield is a passionate person, and I have to say, I really do think the guy gets taken out of context *a lot*. I think he's become somewhat of a target for journalists. He vents often (and usually without a filter) to journalists, who then pick and choose and run a combination of things he said, not necessarily linked by anything. Then it appears in the paper that he thinks Joe Torre doesn't like black people, and Sheff has to make amends and say, "No, that's not what I meant." Granted, he doesn't help his image or his cause when he charges the mound *from first base,* but I think the real Gary Sheffield is a combination of three people: the in-game player, the teammate who seems to get along with everybody in the clubhouse, and the guy we read about in the paper.

I mention Sheffield to point out that while quoting accurately is ideal, it's not enough. Quoting completely and in context is necessary too. The words someone chooses to express himself with are the thumbprints to his personality. If sportswriters collectively agreed to clean up Garry Templeton's catchy phrase, perhaps by attributing to him something like "I see, young man, perhaps I will not be in attendance for such a pitiful mess," people would never have gotten a glimpse of Templeton's charisma and wit and personality, qualities that ultimately have some sort of value in our decision to root for the person and his team. Similarly, reading Sheffield's most inflammatory comments without hearing about his less inflammatory side gives us an inaccurate perception of the player. And we all strive for accuracy. Right?

★

Of all the open spaces that baseball has to offer, the off-season (by off-season I mean the time after your team is out of the race or, better yet, the race has ended and you've won) is by far the largest, and on the surface the most daunting. It is the vastest space of all—between the final out and the great, eternal hope of spring training. How does a baseball fan who has paid such close attention, who has given so much of herself, endure a winter without baseball.

Here's how. First, accept sadness.

Realize that without losing, winning isn't so great. Tell yourself that there's always next year, that hope springs eternal, all that stuff. Basically, acknowledge that once you've learned the difference between a ball and a strike and come to see the sheer skill in hitting to the opposite field, now you have to learn something even more difficult: how to let go. So when your team is seven games out and it's already the first week in September, keep hoping for a miracle (and reading up on the 1964 Cardinals and 2007 Phillies), but in the meantime, steel yourself. I know I have.

The end of a season is bittersweet because once the play-offs start, and your team is not part of it, you're in a situation. One way to deal with it is to curse the opposing team, to develop an ice hockey habit, or to tell any stranger you happen to meet in line for coffee that you hate your home team, that you hate your manager, and that you hate your (insert starting pitcher or slugger who went into a post–All-Star Game slump that he never managed to emerge from). But that would not be healthy. Another way to deal is to root for the team that beat yours, or the team that won the division in which your team competes. That's not a natural reflex. In fact, most people's inclination is obviously to root against the teams that are closest to theirs. Still, you'd be surprised how the playoffs can invert that logic. When the Colorado Rockies beat the Dodgers in 2007, I hated the Rockies. I silently wished them doom every time I saw them, and I started to watch them specifically so I could root against them. But then I had so much fun watching them, I ended up rooting for them.

I'm not saying you should be fickle, or that your love for your home team should be cheap or easily transferable. I'm saying that you should be emotionally invested in your team, but you should also be emotionally invested in the game itself. Of course there are some rivalries that will not result in fans rooting for each other's teams. Yankees fans will never cheer on the Red Sox in a postseason. White Sox fans do not root for the Cubs. In the end, though, the point is not so much whom you root for but that you're rooting at all. No matter who's in the Fall Classic, it's the last dose of baseball you're going to get for a while. Better to enjoy it while it's here, than to miss it when it's gone.

And what about when the game itself is over, when another World Champion has been crowned, tons of ticker tape have been swept up, and baseball is but a chilly memory? There are lots of ways I make it through the depths of a baseball-less winter, and none of them involve Instructional League games in Arizona.

For starters, you can see Ken Burns's documentary, entitled *Baseball,* which I watch just about every off-season to tide me over. I also know people who swear by *Bull Durham* and *Major League* to get them through those cold winter months. Personally I have yet to watch *Field of Dreams* with a man and not have him begin to tear up at the end when Kevin Costner asks his father if he'd like to play catch. (Seriously, I think there's something on the Y chromosome when it comes to that movie, so to any women out there, keep in mind that's a nearly foolproof way to bring out the emotional side in your guy.) I think the key to a good baseball movie is that it has to be fun, but also tinged with that level of nostalgia that we all need to revel in the game. It's a hard line to walk, and while I don't hesitate to bring up the two Kevin Costner baseball movies above, I wouldn't put *For Love of the Game* on the list for just this reason.

Whatever you watch, just make sure that it does justice to the game. There is something so utterly cinematic about baseball that it's hard to make it look bad on film. Maybe it is because of the symmetry. Maybe it is that the game isn't a lateral back and forth. Maybe it is the pace that lends itself to the drama. Whatever it is, I can find something great to be entertained by even in the bad movies made about baseball.

You can also read books about baseball. I've done that, too. To understand statistics, you won't do better than Bill James's *Baseball Abstract*. To understand how modern managers use statistics, check out Michael Lewis's *Moneyball*. Jim Bouton's *Ball Four* will give you a raw, hilarious look at the game, a peek into another era, and a realization that when it comes to misbehavior and all-around nuttiness, today's players have nothing on their counterparts in the sixties. For the soul of the game, one of my favorite baseball novels is *The Entitled* by Frank Deford, which displays a great ability to straddle the line of writing romantically about the game while avoiding cliché. He so captures the essence of baseball that you're at the game in a seat, watching the whole thing unfold. I was also hooked by the fact that the heart of the story is the main character's relationship with his daughter. It probably won't surprise you that I am a sucker for father-daughter stories— especially if they're about baseball.

Two other books worth noting are *A False Spring* by Pat Jordan, the nonfiction account of one young flamethrower's self-immolation in the minors, and *The Natural*, Bernard Malamud's fictional account of a great player and his tragic rise and fall. Both of these do masterful jobs of capturing what makes this game worth coming back to after months of separation.

Wild Pitch   Berg, Moe Berg

Think about this off-season for a moment:

For fifteen seasons, Moe Berg was a backup catcher and infielder, playing for the Brooklyn Robins (a National League team in 1923), Chicago White Sox, Cleveland Indians, Washington Senators, and Boston Red Sox. Berg never played in an All-Star Game, nor did he make the postseason. He hit for a lifetime .243 average and hit 6 home runs. But he did attend Princeton University and Columbia Law School, and he was widely considered the smartest person in the game.

Still, it wasn't until his career ended in 1939 and he joined the Office of Strategic Services during World War II that he became Berg, Moe Berg. Yes, Berg was a spy. His fluency in several languages was an asset, and Berg found himself traveling across most of Eastern Europe gathering information about various anti-Nazi resistance forces that the U.S. government was interested in sponsoring. He also traveled through Germany, interviewing many high-level scientists about that country's race to split the atom.

★

There are other ways to stay involved with the game too. I'm on the Internet a few times a day, following the winter meetings, the hot stove reports. I sometimes look into what the farm team did the year before, who the leaders were in pitching and hitting and steals. I try to predict who might be coming up to the majors in the springtime. I try to track as much as I can in the entire league, what's going on as far as moves and free agency, who's signing whom, who's going on waivers. I especially try to keep track of what teams in my division are doing, because that's going to affect the Dodgers. The latest addition to my off-season regimen is the MLB channel, which offers a constant baseball fix no matter what the month is.

The thing that's important about all of this is to do it casually. I space out my interest over those long winter months because it makes me anticipate the season that much more. And then, when I've done all that—when I've watched the movies and read the books and scoured the Internet for news from the other teams, I do something else: I forget baseball for a few weeks. I know it'll be there when I get back. And it'll be more beautiful than ever.

It's true, the off-season is the biggest, toughest open space that we as fans have to contend with, but it's also true that without it, we'd never be able to realize just how important the game is to us. To throw down a well-worn cliché that's usually used in a totally different context: Absence makes the heart grow fonder. The off-season gives us a built-in time for reflection. It gives us time to appreciate the game and why it's so important.

chapter twelve

The Clothes Make the Blogger

If you come to the fork in the road, take it.
—YOGI BERRA

*L*ike any fan, I have my favorite, regular rooting places. My couch, for one—the seat all the way on the right, with the great sight lines to the television and an iced tea at my side. My seat on the third-base line, for another. Behind my steering wheel, or at my stove, or at my desk, for a few others—wherever I might be listening to a Dodgers radio broadcast.

For the first ten years of my adult life as a fan, I watched and listened in all these locations, and that was enough. Win or lose, I was a fan like most fans, simply following the team, cursing errors and cheering home runs, and it was good. Sure, like any fan, I had my dreams—that one day I might travel to other ballparks or see the inside of a dugout up close, that I might experience the game I loved from a different, more personal seat in the stands. But those were dreams, akin to the fantasies about coconuts and gentle South Pacific breezes that people have been entertaining since they found out about Tahiti.

Of course, every so often you hear stories, tall tales almost of someone who actually moves to the baseball equivalent of the South Pacific and finds paradise. These legends filter back in bits and pieces from the edges of fandom. The old college friends who quit their office jobs, piled into a van, and spent the summer driving across the country, visiting every single major-league ballpark. The guy who decided he wanted to be closer to the game he loved, but instead of simply buying season tickets, he bought a minor-league baseball team. As unexpected as it may seem, he supposedly poured his savings into this new enterprise and found a joy that had eluded him in his previous nine-to-five existence. There was the fable about the former college player who gave up his dream because he had to make a living, and took up teaching and coaching high school, until the day some of his players told him he still had good stuff, and he was always telling them to believe in himself, so why didn't he believe in himself and try out for the big leagues? (He did, and . . . well, watch the Disney movie.)

While these were all extreme cases, the same things

happen every season in smaller ways all around the country as fans express their love for the game with displays that are unbelievable, outrageous, and just plain off-kilter. Fans propose at ballparks. They tattoo their team insignias on their shoulders. They ask that their ashes be scattered over the diamonds where they had lived and (figuratively) died with their heroes.

Buried amid the lore of the game are tales like these, stories of fans who grew so restless that they had to take a new step, a step to become part of the baseball story instead of idly watching from the bleachers. Though some of these steps may seem more excessive than others (I'm pretty sure that getting a tattoo is a much bigger deal than naming your dog Dodger), all fans searching for new ways to come closer to the game share a common ancestry.

I could definitely relate to that impulse, but I knew I'd never be the kind of fan who would paint my house Dodger blue or get married at home plate. And that was okay with me; I didn't need more. I was content to watch at home and dream about driving around the country in a beat-up old motor home with my brother, following the Dodgers and seeing the great ballparks of the land. I thought about this possibility the same way someone in Ponca City, Oklahoma, might think about lounging in Bora-Bora, sipping a mai tai before she threw on her swimsuit and feasted on a freshly caught lobster. I thought about it like the daydream that it was, nothing more.

And then I went to the gift shop at Dodger Stadium to buy a jersey. I know that's not how most stories of dreams come true start out, but that's how mine does. I went into a gift shop at Dodger Stadium to buy a jersey and that led to my line of baseball clothes and that led to my blog and that led to my traveling around the country, seeing (and reporting on) baseball from the inside, and that led, oddly enough, to this book.

Here's what happened: I was at the ballpark for a night game, and we had arrived even earlier than usual. With time to kill, I decided to visit the stadium shop and look for a new piece of Dodger gear to add to my ever-expanding ensemble. I wanted something cute, something to fly the colors, to support the team. No big deal.

I looked. And looked. And looked. I pulled one of those moves where you circle around the store four or five times, combing through racks of clothing as though suddenly, somehow, an item that you previously missed will just magically appear. It didn't. There was nothing there that fit my fashion sense, or my body. It's not that I was being picky. Everything was really boxy; none of the tank tops had undergarments. The only stuff that seemed to be made specifically for women was pink. If there was a single item of Dodger gear for women that wasn't pink, I didn't see it. Last time I checked, Dodger colors were blue and white. Though I'm sure Roy Campanella would have looked quite cute in fuchsia, I'm pretty sure that pink—in all of its varieties—has never been a part of the Dodgers' team colors.

On another night I might have shrugged my shoulders, bought a soda on the way back to my seat, and yelled my head off for the Dodgers. But on this night, for some reason, when

I sat down, instead of focusing on the diamond, I looked around. I craned my neck and scanned the rows of seats behind me. I stood up and got a better view of the fans farther down the line. I stared at the stadium, watching the forty thousand or fifty thousand people around me file into their seats and prepare for the game.

Then it hit me: There were a lot of women at this game.

In fact, if all the women in the stands had been wearing pink, the guy up in the Goodyear blimp probably *would* have thought that pink was one of the Dodgers' colors. Of course only a handful of women were actually wearing pink, and I suspected that most of the women out there felt the same way I did about the pink clothes.

That was when I decided to design some baseball fashions for women.

I can't say that I started doodling designs on a pretzel napkin at the stadium that very night, but it didn't take long for me to realize I was onto something. I talked to my agents at Creative Artists Agency (CAA), and at first they didn't know what to do with my idea. After thinking about it for a while, they introduced me to a guy who worked with Major League Baseball Properties.

The more I talked about this concept with different people, the more my vision for the clothes coalesced. I started to think a lot about being a female fan of a game where everyone usually assumes that the primary fans are men. Contrary to what many people think, my experience of being a female fan is not filled with obstacles. Sure, you have to deal with the occasional jackass guy who assumes you don't know your stats or that you're not serious enough in your devotion. But thankfully, people like that are getting rarer and rarer.

As I began to think about these clothes, I was thinking about the designs not just as a fan, but also as a woman. I was thinking about what being a fan meant to both in a sport that is played by men and managed by men. There hasn't always been much out there for female fans, and for me, planning the designs was as much an exercise in thinking about fandom as it was about the spaghetti straps and halter tops. I considered what was missing from the current options available. I wanted to make a collection that would show a woman could be a woman and fan without having to bear being branded by the "pink letters" on her shirt. I wanted to create clothes that women would want to wear with or without the team logo. I wanted the team logos to compliment the design instead of being the focus.

I wanted to be an intelligent voice representing female baseball fans in their true light. I think that women, with our innate eye for detail and our ability to be instinctually more critical, see the game in a distinctive way. I've long felt that there is a misconception about female sports fans not being feminine. You know what? I am a tomboy. I've always been a tomboy, but that doesn't mean I'm not feminine. I love sports. I can appreciate a pretty slide or a graceful diving catch in the outfield. I can talk numbers with the best of them, and dissect the game with the most critical of them, and get this: I can do it all in a pair of pumps with lip gloss on. I wanted the clothing line to be an extension of this passion for baseball and a reflection of what it means to be a woman who loves baseball.

After a bit of brainstorming and some long nights that ended with lots of paper crumpled up in the trash can, I came up with some ideas and hired a fashion illustrator to get those ideas on paper, and then I went into a room to pitch the concept to five guys from Major League Baseball Properties.

Now, I've taken chances in my life, and I've done some scary things. Everyone has. It's called growing up. But I'll tell you, trying to convince five guys from the most powerful professional sports organization to grant me the licensing for my line of MLB clothes for women, that was scary. I showed them the drawings and talked about the hugely profitable economic niche they were completely missing. I held up an enormous proposal with statistics on how many women come to games and how women are the largest consumers of clothing items. I basically had a book written on why this was a great idea and why that moment was the perfect time to start.

And here are these five businessmen looking at me. I tried looking at it from their perspective, which, I'm pretty sure, was something like this: "Why is this actress trying to get us to let her make a ruffled hoodie?"

I don't know if you're the public-speaking type or not. Clearly I've delivered a lot of lines of scripted dialogue in my time, but that doesn't necessarily mean that I'm the best candidate to pitch a clothing line. There's something about standing in front of a group like that and knowing how skeptical they probably are about what you're saying that makes it harder than any casting call. I wasn't just trying to convince them that I was right for a part. I was trying to convince them that they needed a part in the first place. I've spent a lot of time in front of the camera, but I realized that experience alone would not make this pitch for the MLB women's clothes work.

So I started talking about the Dodgers. I started talking about my dad and Brooklyn and my season tickets and my twenties. I started talking about what the game had meant to me, what it still means to me, and how there are a lot of women out there who have their own connections to baseball through their dads/friends/boyfriends/husbands. I talked about how baseball means a lot to everyone who's a fan; it doesn't matter what gender you are. I talked about how supporting your team with a jersey or a T-shirt is one of the best parts of being a fan, and how I wanted to design clothes that treated women as fans but also treated them as women, because even though women are not on the field, they are just as much a part of the game as men are.

After I finished my rambling speech, there was a brief silence before someone asked, "Where's the pink?"

"No pink," I replied. "All team colors."

"But pink sells," someone else said.

"Pink sells because it is the only thing out there that is specifically made for women. I guarantee if a fan had the option between wearing a boxy pink T-shirt or something that is flattering, made well with a quality fabric, and in her team's colors, she would choose the latter."

I wanted these men to realize that more focus should be spent reaching out to female baseball fans, that we were feeling slightly neglected, and needed a bit of attention that didn't come through a pink filter. As I said during the closing of my pitch, "Pink is a man's answer to female fan apparel. This clothing line is a woman's answer to female fan apparel."

I guess they thought that anyone who loved the game as much as I did was worth taking a risk on, because they gave me the go-ahead and introduced me to G-iii Sports and partners, my manufacturing company.

In retrospect, I don't think they responded as much to my designs as to how much I obviously loved baseball. Ultimately their motivations didn't really matter; what mattered was that they said yes, and walking out of there that day, I saw that I would get the chance to become a fan in a different way, to write my own chapter into the baseball story, and deepen my passion for the game that has meant so much to me.

Wild Pitch Clothes Make the Man

To understand what works in baseball fashion, it's instructive to first look at what most definitely does not work. Take the Chicago White Sox, circa 1976. Please. Two words: short shorts. Right, the White Sox wore short shorts in 1976. Along with knee socks. The effect was men dressed up as a teenage girls' softball team. The experiment lasted three games. The memories will, unfortunately, last forever.

Other, um, advances in baseball uniforms have come more gradually.

The Yankees are often credited with being the first team to add numbers permanently in 1929, though other teams experimented with it as early as 1907. The numbers were to reflect the batting order: Babe Ruth, 3; Lou Gehrig, 4; and so on. The Indians also added numbers permanently in 1929, and they opened their season two days earlier than the Yankees (due to a rainout), but history has given the Yankees the nod on this one. The Yankees haven't done much to their uniform since then. Just a few tweaks here and there, but that's it. Pinstripes. Interlocking NY. Gray road unis with NEW YORK in block lettering. That's tradition for you.

The Dodgers were the first to add a number to the front of their jerseys, in 1952, and they did it in red. Looking back at past Dodgers uniforms, I can only guess that the red is a nod to the original 1901 team, whose base color was red. Other than that, it seems pretty random. But, as we're seeing now, maybe random is the new normal?

The White Sox were also the first team to use a separate jersey for batting practice and warm-ups. They introduced the cooler, more breathable fabric alternatives in 1972, and other teams were quick to follow, um, suit.

And some teams, such as the Phillies, wear special green jerseys if they happen to be playing a spring training game on St. Patrick's Day. The Cincinnati Reds were the first to do this, in 1978.

While the White Sox expressed their fashion courage with the short shorts, their crosstown cousins dared to be different in a subtle fashion.

The C on Chicago Cubs caps is raised like a puffy sticker, while other teams' logos are flat. They also wear their logo on the upper leg of their pants, appearing ever so small. They also wear the restricted logo R on their jerseys, appearing just below the S. While licensing is all over baseball merchandise, trademark logos have been absent from uniforms worn on the field. Not so on the North Side of Chicago. All of this is unique to the Cubs.

The Cubs also wear the National League's patch on their right sleeve. Interesting, because no other team in the Senior Circuit does this, and I can't recall a team in the American League that does this either. Nice touch on the Cubs' part, I think.

In 1972, the Cubs wore pullover jerseys and decided to slap uniform numbers in the middle. That's unique because teams wear them either on the left or on the right. The experiment lasted only for the '72 season, as their uniforms looked more like basketball or football jerseys.

The Cubs also decided to put their numbers in the middle of the C on their helmets. Odd, because teams generally put the player's name and/or number on the *back* of the helmet. Not so for the Cubs.

They wrote their numbers in what looks like white Sharpie smack in the front.

Zippered jerseys, sleeveless jerseys, pleated pants, powder blue uniforms—the Cubs were major fashionistas during the 1930s. Some of the designs that they came up with during this period—namely the powder blues and sleeveless jerseys—are still around today.

Baseball uniforms have changed a lot, to say the least, since the dawn of the game. I even read that there have been more than four thousand different styles since 1876. That's amazing! Who knew men cared so much about fashion! Long-sleeve wool uniforms gave way to three-quarter sleeves, which gave way to short sleeves. Different teams adopted different lengths at different times. It's hard to imagine how hot and scratchy those uniforms had to be during the dog days of summer. But uniforms were either made with 100 percent wool or some sort of combination of wool and cotton flannel. Synthetic materials were a product of World War II, and baseball was quick to sew them into their uniforms. Nylon, Dacron, Orlon—all made for a more comfortable fit during the '50s and '60s. But the real fashion boom happened in the '70s with double-knit fabrics. And boy did those colors pop on television! That's probably why we saw such crazy designs (from the White Sox) back then. Television was in color, and maybe teams wanted to publicize by throwing color all over the place. Thankfully, teams have gone back to a more traditional look.

In the early days of the game, cleats were basically dress shoes with nails pounded through the soles. Ty Cobb was said to slide intentionally with his spikes high for effect, and I'm sure other players were known to do it as well. But it wasn't until the 1960s that spikes really began to change. That's when designers started experimenting more with color, and plastic spikes were soon to follow, and nowadays, especially on artificial turf, sometimes players don't even wear spikes, opting for a flat sole instead. I can see how a flat sole would be good on turf if you were an outfielder who never stepped up to the plate. I mean, what do these guys think is going to happen when they round first? Or second? Or third? They'll slip onto their butts, that's what!

Caps have changed ever so slightly since the beginning of the game. Basically, the crown is fuller now and the brim is extended. Teams have experimented with different designs, but mostly they're pretty standard: solid colors with an initial or logo representing the team's city or team. Back in the old days, to beat the daytime heat, players would wear pieces of cabbage beneath their caps. Apparently, aside from smelling like hell, cabbage keeps your head cool. One day when the fans were particularly caustic, Casey Stengel hid a bird beneath his cap, and when he approached the plate to jeers, he tipped his cap to the fans. The bird flew away, and the fans changed their tone, now cheering for the wacky Stengel.

★

Four months after that meeting with MLB, the clothing line that had been conceived among the racks of pink in the Dodgers store was in stadium shops around the country. It is called Touch, and I thank God every day for the opportunity that MLB gave me. I also thank God for the female fans that supported the line from the beginning and proved me right. I continue to work passionately and solely for them and to make clothes that represent their unique love of the game.

Soon after its appearance I began to promote it in many different ways. As we were strategizing different promotional options, my marketing guy, Mark Jacobsen, mentioned that he thought writing a baseball blog would be a good tool to help the clothing line. He thought it would be a different way to connect with fans and to the game and asked if I had some thoughts to share about baseball.

Asking that question was like asking a bear if she liked honey, or Wimpy if he had developed a taste for hamburgers, or Popeye, spinach. Did I have some thoughts to share about the game? Yeah, you could say that.

At first I assumed I'd just post my musings about the Dodgers and the game. I wanted it to be my own little area to vent and manage from the couch. I didn't have a whole lot of expectations for it, especially since no one outside of my family and friends had ever asked me to talk freely about baseball. If nothing else, I figured it would educate people to the fact that female fans were every bit as diehard as their male counterparts.

Then I actually started blogging, and my already bad case of baseball fever started raging. It didn't take me long to realize that I had a lot to say, not just about the Dodgers but about baseball in general. I started writing about all things related to baseball, which to me ended up being just about everything. Since that day I've written about Manny Ramirez and his dreadlocks, and about the great time I had at the 2008 All-Star Game, and how Andre Ethier should be playing every day, and the bittersweet emotions prompted by the end of the regular season, and snow-outs in Cleveland, and everything else that popped into my mind. I would spend a few hours during the week on the blog and try to get something written by Friday, then would spend the weekend thinking about it and tweaking it a little bit, and on Monday it was up.

The combination of baseball and the Internet is a pretty amazing thing. The more I blogged, the more response I got. Some people agreed with my feelings about Manny; a few didn't. Some people said there was no way it was actually me writing the blog, that I must have hired a ghostwriter (nope, it's all me). A few people said that when it came to baseball, they had no idea what I was talking about, but they loved the way I said it.

The most surprising reaction I got was from the Dodgers

themselves, and it wasn't even directly to me. It happened in August 2007 after I decided to write a letter to Grady Little, who was managing the Dodgers at the time, and post it on the blog.

I wrote:

Hi!

I know you're real busy with the pennant race and all so I won't take up too much of your time. I beg of you, in the future please refrain from batting anyone with a batting average under the Mendoza Line in the CLEANUP spot. I'm all for [Olmedo] Saenz getting the start at first to get some more at bats and give [James] Loney a break, but you may want to consider batting him appropriately for a .185 hitter. Just a suggestion. Call me crazy.

Also, while I have your attention I've got another crazy suggestion: You may want to check out [Andre] Ethier's numbers against lefties (AVG.—.329, OBP—.372, SLG—.466) and start him accordingly. With the way he's been hitting, there is no reason for him not to get the start against lefties unless he is hurt. Crazy right?

> *Thanks,*
> *Alyssa Milano*
> *Dodger fanatic*
> *Peace,*
> *Love,*
> *and Baseball*

Well, the *Los Angeles Times* reprinted the letter, which I figured was cool, because the whole idea was to spread my infectiousness about the game. The post seemed pretty harmless to me, especially since I wasn't saying anything different from what the sports fan blogs were saying, and you could be sure I was less critical than the sports journalists were. I wonder if the Dodgers ever asked T. J. Simers to tone down his column. I guess criticism must cut deeper when it's coming from a celebrity, because to my surprise the Dodgers office called CAA and asked them to ask me to, um, you know, tone things down. CAA said no.

Can you imagine toning me down? I can't either.

On the other side of that same coin, I was amazed to find out that players actually read my blog. Well at least one player did. At the 2007 All-Star Game, where I met Russell Martin, my current favorite Dodger, I was floored when he told me that he was a reader. He actually asked me, "How do you know so much about baseball?" I told him I read a lot, watched a lot, and had a great brother and father, who were knowledgeable about the game and taught me well.

It had never occurred to me that players might be interested to read what I had to say about the game. Knowing that there was a chance that they were reading it added a bit of stress. Part of the beauty behind the Internet is that you can express yourself with what seems to be a bit of anonymity and freedom. To know that the blog was finding its way to players' computer screens upped the stakes a bit, but it also gave me an opportunity to say things that I hoped they might read. I liked knowing that I could share a fan's perspective on what they do and how much we appreciate all their hard work.

Such was the case when the Dodger fans started getting frustrated with Andruw Jones's performance and booing him every time he stepped up to the plate. I wanted him to know that there were Dodger fans out there who believed in him and his ability to turn things around. Unfortunately, he wasn't able to turn things around. I don't have any doubt that his struggles were just as much mental as they were physical. Maybe even more so. And the booing didn't help.

For most of the 2007 season things went on like this, as I added posts, promoted the clothing line, and always signed off "Peace, Love, and Baseball." One day out of the blue TBS called and asked if I wanted to do some on-air reporting. I thought about it for about a twentieth of a second. My only concern was that even though I love the game and felt like I knew the game, I didn't want it to come across as though I were some kind of sports commentator. Because I'm not. I'm a fan who was given an opportunity to share her love of the game with everyone and anyone. I'm a fan who wanted to help get other people excited about baseball, but I was not looking to be the second coming of Mel Allen (though I do think we need to see more women calling games). I was a fan who stumbled onto a good idea that resulted in a terrific chance and the opportunity to travel to different ballparks around the country. Now there's a Disney movie.

All of a sudden I had amazing access to players, and to stadiums that I'd always heard about and seen on television but had never visited. I signed the wall inside the Green

Monster in Fenway Park, where families pass down season tickets from generation to generation, and some of the veterans tell me they look up from their positions sometimes and can actually watch children turn into adults and parents. I was in the new stadiums, where everything is bright and shiny, and the old parks where you can see the accumulated dust of the game piled up in the corners. I was talking to peanut vendors and beer guys with southern accents and Yankee accents and no discernible accents at all, and they were all telling me the same thing—how much the people who come to their park love the game and the game loves them back, too. I was in the ball humidor at Coors Field. I was opening the roof at Chase Field. I was in the dugout talking to Trevor Hoffman, and he was teaching me where to hold the ball if I'm throwing a changeup. I was talking to Theo Epstein about the season and if it had unfolded the way he'd thought it would. I was talking about all kinds of inside-baseball stuff, but that was okay because for once I got to use the term "inside baseball" and actually be inside baseball.

 **More Than Human**

In between innings they appear in their furry costumes and jump around while the players warm up. They mock the umpires, taunt the opposing team, and try to provoke the fans into cheering. Or booing. Basically, any reaction to keep the fans entertained is currency for a mascot.

Perhaps no mascot does this better and is more famous than the San Diego Chicken. He reached icon status when the *Sporting News* ranked him among the Top 100 Most Powerful People in Sports of the 20th Century. He shares space with Babe Ruth and Muhammad Ali, among others on the list. Not bad for a guy who one day decided to wear his chicken suit in public.

I'm not really sure *what* the Philly Phanatic is, but fans love him. He's got that Philadelphia wit, which is to say he *loves* pissing off the umpires and other teams. (Philly fans once booed Santa Claus. That's cold.) The Phanatic is good at provoking an opposing player by mimicking his warm-up throws, then curtsying like a little girl. Usually the player laughs; sometimes the player chases the Phanatic off the field, and the fans are left wondering if that was scripted or spontaneous rage on the player's part.

In this day and age, I often overhear fans wishing ill on mascots. People seem to delight in the embarrassment or misfortune of someone else. Schadenfreude, I think it's called. German word. It's a shame and an unfortunate pimple on the face of America, but when you willingly strap yourself into a pair of Rollerblades, grab hold of the tow line, and give the okay for the high-speed golf cart to take off, you can't be surprised when you lose control and break your leg. Just like the Seattle Mariners mascot in the old Kingdome. The video is all over the Internet. If you haven't seen it, it is, admittedly, funny in its absurdity, but still painful to watch. C'mon, dude crashed into a wall and broke his leg. In costume. Ugh, the horror.

And then there was the beheading of a mascot in Cincinnati. Again, our hero stepped onto the back of a golf cart, the driver sped away like a bank robber, and the poor Red Stocking fell off, and landed in such a way that the costume head popped off and rolled into the outfield grass. It was baseball's version of Sleepy Hollow, to the horror of little boys and girls at the Great American Ballpark and across Ohio.

★

And when it was all over, I got to come back to the Dodgers, to my seats on the third-base line. Sitting in those seats and watching a game, I don't doubt that I could have lived out my life as a fan on the third-base line, on my couch, and listening to the Dodgers on the radio. I don't doubt that hundreds of thousands if not millions of fans are loyal, and fierce, and never need to do anything other than support the home team.

Some people book a flight to Bora-Bora and live for a week

in a thatched hut, and some people get a tattoo, or propose at Wrigley Field. I never thought my fandom would really go anywhere beyond my yelling loud and long for the Boys in Blue. And then something funny happened. I went looking for something cute to wear, and I saw a lot of pink.

chapter *thirteen*

The Final Out

A man travels the world over in search of what he needs, and returns home to find it.
—GEORGE MOORE

*I*magine this for a moment:

The entire Milano clan in New York for the 2008 All-Star Game. It was only the second time we had all been together in New York since my immediate family made the move to Los Angeles over twenty years ago. The trip was overwhelming for many reasons. We were at Yankee Stadium for the last time before they tore it down. I got to stand next to my father as they introduced Reggie, the hero of my youth, as part of the opening ceremony celebrating the Hall of Famers. Reggie took the field with Yogi Berra and Goose

Gossage. And as I looked at my father, my mother, and my brother, with tears and goose bumps I realized, "We all ended up right where we began. Packed into the stands of a New York team, everyone cheering together."

If that picture isn't enough for you, add this to it: fifteen innings, four hours and fifty minutes, the longest game in All-Star history.

I think the consummate Yankee, Derek Jeter, put it the best when he said of the game, "It seemed like the Stadium didn't want it to end." I have to say the Stadium and I were in agreement about that.

But when all was said and done the game did end, and a few months later so did the Stadium. Some parks just know how to say good-bye. Love it or hate it, Yankee Stadium was one of those parks. Ebbets Field was also like that; so were the Polo Grounds and Comiskey Park. Though Yankee Stadium had changed a lot since the twenties when Ruth and Gehrig ruled the lineup, there's no denying the sheer amount of history there, piled layer upon layer like an ancient city. Every time a dynasty ended, it seemed, a new one would begin, starting from the ground up and building on what had come before.

I try not to long *too* hard for those seasons of an age past; still, some part of me will probably *always* long for those old days. When life and baseball were simple. When there were no worries. When the game was pure. I will long for those days my father speaks of, and I wonder if *my* kids will some-day long for the days I speak of. What will I speak of? I have no doubt that the glories of years past will be revisited by future generations. Maybe by then it will just be back to the way it was. History repeats itself. All things are cyclical. Maybe society as a whole will come full circle. Maybe baseball will come full circle.

A year now for me is one-thirty-sixth of my life. I am thirty-six years old. Just writing that seems odd. I am thirty-six years old. I still wear my Dodger blue retainer to sleep. I still get pimples. I will always be grateful for my family. I will always be grateful for baseball.

Baseball is that odd constant that's always growing and changing yet somehow is always the same. I guess in that respect it really is like life. You know when you were in your twenties and archaic people over thirty would say things like "Wait until you are in your thirties. When you are in your thirties your whole body aches" or "The older you get, the more time speeds up"? And you probably sat there in all your youth-induced, indestructible glory, and thought to yourself, "Not me" or "Blasphemy. Time can't just speed up, archaic thirty-two-year old person," much like I did. Well, I have news for those who haven't reached thirty yet, and I am sure those over thirty can confirm these two things:

A Everything does hurt after a certain age. I mean really. What gives with all the aches and pains? I wake up now and wonder how I hurt myself sleeping.

B Time really does speed up. Well, not literally, but it sure does feel that way.

If you think about it, when you were little, let's say seven years old, one year was one-seventh of your entire life. Obviously, when you get older, one year is a smaller portion of your existence, so it feels like it takes less time to complete a year, or to wait a year for that matter. Time feels like it has sped up.

Remember when you were seven and it seemed like forever for your next birthday to arrive? Time just seemed to crawl at this amazingly consistent, bearable, lovely pace. I had time to do everything I wanted to do when I was seven. I could wake up, have breakfast, go to school, come home, play, do homework, play some more, do a performance, come home, and read a bedtime story before it was time to sleep. I remember being a teenager, and thinking anything even resembling responsibility seemed so far in the distance. "In the year 2000 I will be twenty-eight," I would marvel with the naïveté of a girl with no clue. I remember innocence. It almost had its very own smell, a blend of cotton candy and fresh-cut grass.

Most people probably see time going by faster as a bad thing. Me, I'm a glass-is-half-full kind of girl. The fact that time feels faster just means the off-season goes by more quickly. Baseball will never make the passing of years easy, but it does make it easier.

I look back on my life thus far and think of the many paths I could have taken. I remember being nineteen. Mike Scioscia was a Dodger, and I was out of work after years of stability on *Who's the Boss?* I had distinct choices when I was nineteen. Life could have gone in an entirely different direction for me had I made different choices. After all, we've seen what happens to most young people in the entertainment industry. It's not an easy existence. Young actors have strangers coddling them constantly and saying yes to their every whim. There's a sudden influx of ridiculous amounts of money, and even though you can't touch that money until you're eighteen, you know it's there. And at a time when you mostly just want to be invisible to make your growing-pain mistakes in secrecy, the media are watching your every move, almost waiting for you to fail so that they have a story to sell.

On top of all this, I also had to deal with a certain amount of guilt that accompanied being successful at a young age. The guilt that my parents gave up their dreams, friendships, and the only life they knew to make *my* triumphs a possibility. The guilt that my brother had to deal with having a famous sister. It was not easy, but thank God I had them to remind me what is important in life.

Looking back on those years, there's no question in my mind that there was definitely a path of self-destruction I could have taken. We've all seen it happen. More often than not, the clichés of Hollywood are clichés for a reason. It's a magical place, where dreams are made, blah blah blah. The bad news is that with those shiny, happy tales come those that are not so pleasant, as kids are pushed to their limits by fame and having to grow up much too fast. There are a lot of different ways for a young star to cope with all those feelings, and a lot of them are not good.

Having said that, no matter how trying the situation was back then, if I was given the option of going to clubs to drink and party or going to some sporting event, *any* sporting event, I chose the sporting event every time. And luckily, I had a family that not only encouraged me in my choices, but bought the tickets and came with me. They have kept me grounded in ways I can never express. Whether it was my mom making sure dinner was on the table at six o'clock sharp every night, my brother pointing out my zits by asking, "Wart in the hell is that on your face?" or my dad teaching me the infield fly rule (the specifics of which still give me trouble sometimes), they were always somehow there to break my fall. To this day, the only place I really feel safe from the madness and stresses of this crazy industry is at home, on their cozy couch, which thankfully isn't as itchy as the couch from my childhood.

I believe everyone is on his or her own path. I believe some monumental flags have already been mapped out by some higher power. The rest of life you fill in along the way while collecting experience and making choices that lead to soulful learning. Somehow, we fulfill whatever growth we were supposed to accomplish. It's like a Global Positioning System (GPS, but I much prefer the entire name to the acronym). You start at a specific place, you know your final destination, and even though there's a recommended course, you never know what is going to come up that may make you take an alternative route. Sometimes you take the freeway. Sometimes you take the streets because of traffic. Sometime you choose to take the long way home just because. I took the road less traveled, and it has taken me all the way from Brooklyn to the place I am in now, with many pit stops in between.

Baseball is a big part of what connects those years to now—from the itchy couch to its more comfortable replacement. It pops up routinely throughout my life—sometimes as a bit player and sometimes as a central character. As such, baseball is a way to mark the passing of time. It has the ability to take you back to a specific day, to mark it in your mind and brand it there forever.

On June 20, 2004, my brother and I had something up our sleeves. We planned on surprising my dad with a special Father's Day gift. We had been planning and planning for weeks. We didn't tell him where we were going, although I am pretty sure that after we picked him up and got on the road, he knew we were headed to the stadium. But what he didn't know was that in the trunk of our car were three baseball gloves.

The Dodgers were playing the Yankees that day, adding more sentimentality to what we had planned. We parked our car.

"We're here early," my dad said as we piled out of the car and I opened the trunk to pull out the gloves.

"Here, Dad. You're going to need your glove today," I said while handing him his.

"Huh? Why?" he asked.

"You'll see," my brother said.

We walked a different route to the stadium than we normally did. Dad was confused.

"Where are we going?" he asked.

"You'll see, Dad! Shh!"

My mother meanwhile was behind us, giggling. Looking

back, I am surprised she kept the secret. My mom is bad at keeping secrets when it comes to gifts.

We were met at the gate of the stadium by a rep from the team who was in on the whole surprise. She walked us into the park and then onto the field, where there were thousands of sons and daughters playing catch with their dads.

"Put on your glove, Dad," my brother said.

"Oh my God," my dad said. "This is amazing."

My brother was twenty-one at the time and I was thirty-one. I wish I could say there were lots of other adult children playing catch with their fathers. There weren't. There were some but the three of us were definitely in the minority. We laughed at that fact. We laughed a lot. And we played catch on the field at Dodger Stadium.

When it was time to leave the field, my dad grabbed our hands and we walked together. I will never forget that day. The Dodgers beat the Yankees 5–4. Lima got the win.

But just as baseball can take you back to a specific day, it can also take you back to a general time. The summer of your first kiss or the fall that you went away to college. The spring of your wedding or the October that you met your husband. For all of those times and countless others, baseball is the noise coming from the TV in the corner while the vacuum is on and the centerpiece of a summer well spent on the third-base line.

For as much as baseball is about the past, it's also about the present, and that's why, year in and year out, I come back to it. I come back to the game that taught me the only way to be happy was to be where I am. Without baseball I'm not sure

I ever would have learned to be in the moment. To focus on what's in front of me, and tune out the background noise. To ignore the sound of the vacuum cleaner and just focus on the game itself.

A big part of what allows me to be in the moment is the community that surrounds the game. While the Internet has opened up all kinds of baseball possibilities for me (including this book), it can also make the game a more disconnected and impersonal event. This is a big part of why I'm a season ticket holder. I go to games not just for the baseball, but for the people, and for the feeling of community I get while there. My neighborhood is Dodger Stadium. My neighbors are the fans that sit in my section. There is the family of six that sits two rows down. I've known their daughter since she was thirteen, and last season I watched her go off to college in Boston.

"Promise me you won't become a Red Sox fan," I said when she told me she was leaving soon.

"I won't," she said. I've kept tabs on her through her parents, and if what they say is true, she's kept to her word.

In the row right in front of me is a couple named Frank and Kendace. I call them Uncle Frank and Aunt Kendace. They were gone for a while in the middle of the 2008 season, and I started to worry about them. When they returned, they told me they had been in Asia traveling for business. They brought me back a teapot and tea.

Then there's Cort and Nancy, who sit next to me. They have a young daughter whom I gave a Touch jacket to, but in less than a year, she has almost grown out of it.

When the end of every season inevitably rolls around, all of us—all of these disparate groups of people who would probably never have passed each other on the street, let alone spoken—check with one another to make sure that we will all buy our tickets in the same place, so that we're all together again.

At every stadium across the country, relationships like these are made. If you do it long enough, you end up making a new life for yourself right there in the stadium. It becomes a home away from home, where you can take your shoes off and watch the game, so long as you don't let your feet touch the floor. (On second thought, maybe you should just leave your shoes on.)

I've created my own Flatbush Avenue right in the middle of downtown L.A. Dodger Stadium is my Ebbets Field. It might not be as romantic as all the stories I heard tossed around the kitchen table when I was younger. It may not be surrounded with egg creams and stickball and baseball cards in the spokes of bikes. But it houses pieces of my history and in the end, that's what matters to me.

Peace,

Love,

and Baseball.

Glossary

Baseball has its own geekspeak, its own parlance. Not knowing the lingo can be likened to spending a weekend in a foreign country, being asked to answer questions about the Bush doctrine, and blind dates. In other words: awkward. By no means is this list exhaustive, but here's a quick-reference decoder guide to get you through those hard times.

A

ace—A team's best starting pitcher.

ALCS—American League Championship Series; the second-round, best-of-seven playoffs in the AL.

ALDS—American League Division Series; the first-round, best-of-five playoffs in the AL.

alley—The space between outfielders; also called the **gap.**

All-Star break—Three-day vacation in July for players who didn't make the All-Star team.

All-Star Game—A game in which the two league's best, as decided by fans, play for World Series home field advantage. Also called the Midsummer Classic.

Arizona Fall League—An instructional league for the top prospects in the majors.

arm slot—The location and angle of a pitcher's arm at the point he releases the ball.

around the horn—After an out, infielders toss the ball to each other before handing it back to the pitcher.

assist—Recording an out by throwing the ball.

B

backdoor—A term referring to late movement of a pitch, typically on a slider.

backstop—Either the screen behind home plate or the catcher.

balk—An illegal movement by the pitcher intending to deceive the base runner; as a penalty all runners advance one base no matter where they are on the diamond.

Baltimore chop—A ground ball that hits in front of (or off of) home plate and takes a large hop over an infielder's head.

base on balls—A walk.

battery—The combination of pitcher and catcher.

beaned—Getting hit by the pitch; typically refers to getting hit in the head.

big leagues—Synonym for major leagues.

blue—Another word for the umpire.

bow tie—A fastball, high and inside.

box score—A statistical game-action recap.

BP—Abbreviation for batting practice.

Bronx cheer—When the crowd boos.

brushback—The term for a pitch that comes close to hitting the batter.

bunt—When the batter holds his bat over the plate and taps at the incoming pitch.

bush league—Unprofessional conduct.

C

Cactus League—Spring-training games in Arizona.

can of corn—A routine fly ball.

changeup—A pitch thrown slower than a fastball, intended to mess with a hitter's timing.

check swing—When a batter starts to swing at a pitch but pulls back before the ball reaches the plate.

chin music—A fastball, high and inside.

closer—The relief pitcher used exclusively to record the save and preserve the win.

crew chief—The head umpire.

cup of coffee—A brief appearance in the majors.

curveball—A pitch that swerves and drops as it reaches the plate.

cutoff man—The infielder who relays the throw from the outfield.

cutter—A fastball that moves away from a right-handed batter if thrown by a right-handed pitcher; also known as a cut-fastball.

Cy Young Award—Annual award given to the best pitcher of each league, decided by the sportswriters.

D

day-night doubleheader—An afternoon game followed by a night game with separate admissions; also called a split doubleheader.

Deadball Era—The first twenty years of the twentieth century, when the ball was not as lively and home runs were not as frequent.

decision—A win or loss for a pitcher.

defensive indifference—When the team in the field elects not to throw the ball when a base runner steals.

designated hitter (DH)—The player who hits for the pitcher but does not play the field. Used in the American League only, since 1973.

deuce—Curveball.

double play—When the fielding team records two outs on one play.

double steal—Two base runners steal at the same time.

double switch—Replacing the pitcher and a fielder at the same time; a strategy typically used in the National League, late in the game, if the pitcher's turn in the batting order is due in the next frame. The incoming fielder will bat in the outgoing pitcher's slot, and the new pitcher will bat in the outgoing fielder's spot, presumably further down the order.

drag bunt—When a left-handed batter squares to bunt and starts moving toward first base before the ball reaches the plate.

ducks on the pond—Runners in scoring position; especially with the bases loaded.

dying quail—A weak fly ball.

E

earned run average (ERA)—The average number of runs a pitcher would surrender over the course of a game had he been kept in for the full nine innings.

error—A fielder's botched play.

eye black—The black war paint players wear beneath their eyes during day games, ostensibly to reduce the sun's glare.

F

Fall Classic—World Series.

fall off the table—A curveball that drops as though it were, well, *falling off a table*.

farm team—A minor-league team.

fastball—A pitch that travels fast, intended to be straight, lauded if it has some movement.

fielder's choice—Term for when the fielder opts to retire a base runner instead of the hitter.

finesse pitcher—A pitcher who lacks a strong fastball but manages to succeed by effectively changing speeds with excellent location. Think Greg Maddux.

fireman—A team's closer or late-inning relief pitcher.

five-man rotation—Term for the five starters on a team's pitching staff. Teams have experimented with three- and four-man rotations, but five is considered the industry standard, as it allows enough recovery time for pitchers between starts without too much downtime.

five-tool player—A player who can hit for average, hit for power, run, field, and throw.

flamethrower—A pitcher who throws fastballs at very high speed.

flashing leather—When a fielder makes a great catch.

foul poles—Those yellow poles down the right- and left-field lines with vertical flags extending on the fields are the foul poles. They are in play, so if a batted ball hits one, it's a home run.

frame—As a noun, a frame is another word for an inning. As a verb, it means to catch a borderline strike in such a way as to make the umpire *think* it was a strike.

free agent—A player who is available to sign with any team.

frozen rope—A hard-hit line drive.

full count—Three balls, two strikes.

fungo—A long, thin bat used to hit during practice.

G

gap—The open space between outfielders, also called the **alley**.

golden sombrero—The ignominy of striking out four times in one game.

Gold Glove—Annual award for the best fielder at his position, in each league, as voted by managers and coaches.

grand slam—A home run with the bases loaded.

Grapefruit League—Spring-training games played in Florida.

ground-rule double—A fair ball that bounces out of play or is touched by a fan, resulting in an automatic double.

H

hanger—A curveball or slider that doesn't break, rendering it ineffective and allowing the batter to time it perfectly.

heater—Fastball.

high heat—A high fastball.

hit-and-run—Perhaps the phrase is out of order and should be called the run-and-hit. Anyway, the runners go in motion before the ball is hit, though it's not intended to be a straight steal, so as to pull the fielders out of position to cover the bag, thus opening the field through which the batter can poke a hit and the runners can take an extra base.

hitting for the cycle—When a batter hits a single, double, triple, and home run (not necessarily in that order) in a single game.

homestand—The series of games at the home team's field.

hook slide—A type of slide in which the runner slides past the bag, in order to avoid the tag, and reaches the base with his back foot.

hot corner—Third base.

hot stove—Term for the off-season action including player trades and acquisitions.

I

infield fly rule—It is an automatic out if a pop-up is hit with less than two outs, runners on first and second (or the bases are loaded) and the umpire deems that the pop-up can be caught by an infielder. The rule is to prevent fielders from intentionally not catching the ball, forcing an easy double play or triple play.

in the hole—The batter following the **on-deck** batter.

J

journeyman—A player who has played for a variety of teams over the course of his career.

junior circuit—American League, established in 1901, twenty-five years after the National League.

junkballer—A pitcher who has neither power nor finesse, but who has found success in off-speed and breaking pitches.

K

K—Scorecard mark for strikeout swinging.

Я—Strikeout looking.

Keystone—Second base.

L

lollipop—A soft throw with a high arc.

M

magic number—The number of games left for a contending team to clinch a postseason berth.

Mendoza Line—Refers to a .200 batting average. Named after Mario Mendoza, who batted below .200 five times between 1974 and 1982.

minor leagues—The system in which all big-league clubs grow their prospects.

Modern Era—1893 to the present.

Most Valuable Player (MVP)—Award given to one player from each league annually, as decided by the sportswriters.

N

Negro Leagues—Before baseball was desegregated in 1947, the Negro Leagues included teams made up mostly of African Americans.

NLCS—National League Championship Series; the second-round, best-of-seven playoffs in the NL.

NLDS—National League Division Series; the first-round, best-of-five playoffs in the NL.

no-decision—When the starting pitcher does not figure in the winning or losing of his game.

no-hitter—A game in which a pitcher does not allow any hits.

O

Oh-*Fer*—A term referring to an unsuccessful series of at bats or games, as in "The batter went 0–for–4 on Saturday."

on-base percentage (OBP)—The number of times a batter makes it on base (after discounting fielders' choices and errors) divided by his number of plate appearances.

on deck—Next to bat.

opposite field—The half of the baseball diamond away from most batters' natural power. For right-handed batters, right field is the opposite field. For left-handed batters, left field is.

P

painting the black—When a pitcher throws the ball over the edge of the plate.

passed ball—A ball the catcher should have caught, allowing the base runners to advance, though not an official error.

perfect game—A game in which the pitcher allows no base runners.

phenom—A player who surprises scouts, fans, and managers by displaying excellence at a young age. Pronounced PHEE-nom.

pickoff—A term referring to the pitcher's throw to a base from which the runner is leading.

pinch hitter—A player who enters a game specifically to bat for another player.

pinch runner—Same as a pinch hitter, except to run the bases.

plate appearance—Each time a player completes a turn batting.

pop-up—A ball hit very high that stays in the infield.

Pythagorean expectation—A Bill James formula designed to predict the winning percentage of a team based on how many runs the team scores and allows. It's interesting to compare a team's theorem with its actual winning percentage to see if it is over- or underachieving.

Q

quality start—When the starting pitcher goes six innings without giving up more than three earned runs.

R

round-tripper—Home run.

rubber game—The deciding game of a series.

Rule 5 Draft—Intended to prevent teams from stockpiling prospects on their minor-league rosters, the Rule 5 Draft allows teams to select players not currently on a forty-man roster. Naturally, there are many complicated exemptions.

S

sacrifice bunt—The hitter bunts with the intent of getting thrown out at first in order to advance the base runners.

sacrifice fly—A fly ball hit to the outfield for an out, allowing the runner on third to score.

safety squeeze—The batter squares to bunt, and the runner on third breaks for home as soon as the ball is put into play.

senior circuit—National League, established in 1876, twenty-five years before the American League.

set-up man—A relief pitcher who enters the game in the seventh or eighth inning, intending to preserve the lead for the closer.

shag—Fielding fly balls during batting practice.

slider—A pitch that breaks laterally and down, with more speed than a curveball but slower than a fastball.

slugger—A batter who tends to hit for extra bases, especially home runs.

slugging percentage—The number of total bases a batter earns (excluding walks) divided by the number of batting opportunities.

southpaw—Left-handed pitcher.

spring training—Preseason, between roughly February 15 and March 30.

stretch—The pitcher uses a shorter motion to the plate with runners on base.

submariner—A pitcher who throws sidearm to the extent that his delivery looks underhand.

suicide squeeze—The runner on third breaks for home at the pitcher's first movement, and the hitter squares to bunt moments before he makes contact. It is insane and dangerous and awesome to see in the works.

switch hitter—A batter who can hit from both sides of the plate.

T

tag up—The base runner must wait for the fly ball to be caught before he can advance to the next base.

take a pitch—A phrase for not swinging at a pitched ball.

tater—A home run.

Texas Leaguer—A bloop hit that drops between an infielder and an outfielder.

Tommy John surgery—Elbow-ligament replacement surgery, made famous by the All-Star Dodger pitcher.

Triple Crown (batting)—When a player leads his league at season's end in the categories of hitting percentage, home runs, and runs batted in. The last batting Triple Crown winner was Carl Yastrzemski of the Boston Red Sox in 1967.

Triple Crown (pitching)—When a pitcher leads his league at season's end in the categories of earned run average, wins, and strikeouts. The last pitching Triple Crown winner was Jake Peavy of the San Diego Padres in 2007.

twinight doubleheader—A doubleheader in which the first game starts in the late afternoon or evening.

twin killing—A **double play**.

W

walk-off—A game-winning hit in the bottom of the ninth or in extra innings.

warning track—The redbrick dust track that encircles the entire field as a warning to fielders drifting for a fly ball that the wall is only a couple of steps away.

WHIP (walks plus hits per innings pitched)—The number of hits allowed by a pitcher plus the number of walks allowed by the same pitcher, divided by innings pitched.

wild card—The postseason berth for the best second-place team in each league.

wild pitch—A pitch that misses the catcher's target, gets away from the catcher, and allows the base runners to advance.

windup—The delivery a pitcher uses to throw the ball to the catcher when there are no runners on base.

World Series—The final round of the postseason and the reason all baseball players put on a uniform.

Acknowledgments

Special thanks to Joe Torre for agreeing to be a part of this project and for deciding to come across the country to manage the team that I love.

This book would not have been possible without the work and brain of Steve Friedman. His tireless efforts are reflected in every "Wild Pitch."

My editor, Matt Harper, gave me the courage and guidance to just keep writing. His constant support is reflected on every single page.

And many thanks to the people at William Morrow for believing in me and giving me this great opportunity.